Just Imagine

To Madeleine

Just Imagine

Creative ideas for writing

James Carter

David Fulton Publishers
London

David Fulton Publishers Ltd
Ormond House, 26-27 Boswell Street, London WC1N 3JZ
www.fultonpublishers.co.uk

First published in Great Britain in 2002 by David Fulton Publishers

British Library Cataloguing in Publication Data
A catalogue record for this book is available from the British Library.

ISBN 1-85346-805-3

Designed and typeset by Kenneth Burnley, Wirral, Cheshire
Printed and bound in Great Britain by Bell and Bain Ltd, Glasgow

Contents

COMPACT DISC
Features five instrumental pieces and three soundscapes
(see Music chapter for track listings)

Introduction

CREATING IDEAS AND WRITING WITH THIS BOOK

In truth, it's never really a case of having to *just* imagine - imagining, and the sourcing of ideas are fundamental to creative writing, and can even be a challenge at times to those who write for a living. All of us, on occasion, whether child or adult, amateur or professional, experienced or otherwise, need stimuli to spark off ideas for creative writing.

Hardly a day goes by when teachers do not ask their classes to produce some form of writing: poems, stories, autobiographical writing or informative pieces. We expect children to function as endless wells of creativity. Admittedly, children do not have the inhibitions that adults frequently have, yet they do need nurturing, direction and support as well as frameworks and models for their creativity - and this book seeks to help with these. In addition, *Just Imagine* aims to be a versatile and flexible resource that will offer teachers practical and stimulating creative writing activities that can be put into immediate use in the classroom. Each of the activities provided can easily be adapted according to the specific needs of pupils and classrooms and even used for *ad hoc* activities. The bulk of the material in each chapter - including the writing workshops - is directed at children, and can hence be read out loud to a class or small group.

The poet John Foster has, perhaps, the most definitive and satisfactory response to the perennial question 'Where do you get your ideas from?', by commenting that his ideas derive from a combination of three sources: imagination, observation and experience. This book encourages children to actively call upon all three of these in a range of workshops within the following genres:

- fiction - including short stories, mini-sagas, monologues, short dramatic sketches, comic strips, picture books and screenplays;
- poetry - including free verse, rhyming verse and syllabic poetry;
- non-fiction - including autobiographical writing, journalism and travel writing.

It seeks to enable children to:

- enjoy their creativity;
- develop confidence with their writing;
- improvise on initial ideas and themes;
- work with a range of media and stimuli;
- deepen their understanding of the creative process;
- discover their own preferred methods of writing;
- explore a range of literary forms and genres within fiction, non-fiction and poetry;
- appreciate the interconnectedness of media;
- discover their own literary 'voices';
- follow certain structured creative writing pieces; yet
- have the freedom to follow their own creative paths.

Perhaps the most important of all the factors above is that children need to feel confident about their writing, as author Michael Morpurgo stresses:

> Confidence is everything to me as a writer. I love helping to give children confidence in encouraging them to write, and to make them all feel that they've got something to say, and that writing is not that difficult or something to worry about, that it's natural. I tell children that they shouldn't overwork a piece of writing. One thing I say to them which is not always popular with teachers, is that when they're getting their ideas onto paper they should *tell* it down onto the page, and should not worry about spelling, punctuation and grammar - just tell it down as if they're speaking it. Then later you go back to it and get the spelling and everything right - and that stage is important too, or otherwise the story can't be properly communicated to other people.

Confidence in a workshop environment means that the children are feeling positive about exploring their ideas, and feeling comfortable enough to write down any thoughts or images that might come to them as they are brainstorming. As a writer you never know what ideas you are going to use at a later stage, so you have to be prepared to write down literally anything that comes to mind. In the classrom this can only be achieved if children have no inhibitions, and they are also concentrating on the creative rather than the formal aspects of writing (as Michael Morpurgo stresses above), which can be properly addressed at a later editing stage. Above all, children's confidence comes from feeling that their ideas and writing are of value, that they as writers are respected by the classroom teacher. To this end, it is important to regularly publish children's writing.

Publishing helps to give a purpose, a direction, a goal, as well as a reward to writing. Above all, it increases motivation and helps boosts self-esteem. Young writers need to see that there is a product as well as a process to their writing, which can be published in a variety of ways, including:

- class/year group/school anthologies - as themed or miscellaneous anthologies;
- displays - in the classroom, in the corridors, in the hall, at the entrance to the school, or as 'poem/story of the week' on notice boards;

- school website/other websites (see 'Useful Websites', p. 111);
- poems in particular can be recorded onto audio cassette or video. Likewise, performances of poems - perhaps to coincide with a visiting writer - can be recorded in this way;
- poems/stories can be read/performed to other year groups;
- local newspapers/local radio stations, which may be happy to broadcast recordings done by the school or may invite pupils to record poems/stories in their studios;
- school magazines.

Children will find that the more they write, the more ideas they will have, and that these won't only come to them during writing workshops. Benjamin Zephaniah experiences this with his poetry:

> I sometimes feel that I'm writing all the time, that I'm always collecting ideas, whatever I'm doing. There's a difference between creating a poem and writing a poem. I create poems anywhere and everywhere - like when I'm jogging - but the actual writing happens here in the office.

For this very reason, it is useful for children to keep notebooks or folders in which they can collect and source all their ideas and potential material.

The soundtrack composer Barrington Pheloung believes that 'composition is a form of improvisation'. The same principle applies to creative writing. Taking an idea and developing it is actually a form of improvisation. To improvise, one needs to feel comfortable and confident (that word again!) - both of which come from regular practice as well as full teacher support.

This book takes three different though interconnected media by which to generate and explore creative writing - 'Text and Themes', 'Images' and 'Music' - and a chapter is dedicated to each of these. Each chapter opens with general advice on using that particular media for creative writing and then goes on to explain how to approach the workshop activities.

The 'Text and Themes' chapter contains a range of text extracts such as poetry, prose fiction, drama text and autobiographical writing. The prose extracts derive from a number of literary genres, including realism and fantasy. This chapter is divided into seven theme-centred sub-sections: memories, dreams, school life, friendships, outsiders, journeys and time. The writing workshop activities throughout this chapter relate to both the text extracts and the central themes. 'Text and Themes' also contains exclusive interview clips from various popular contemporary children's authors - including David Almond, Malorie Blackman, Berlie Doherty and Jacqueline Wilson - in which they discuss favoured themes in their writing. Each themed section also has a series of 'Discussion Points' which can help children to consider the subject area before any writing takes place; also, it will allow them to share their viewpoints and to listen to others, which, in itself is often an invaluable source of ideas.

The 'Images' chapter features photographs, paintings, artwork and illustrations by a range of professional artists, photographers and children's illustrators, as well as some pre-twentieth-century works from Tate Britain. The introduction to this chapter gives a range of general workshop activities relating to methods of using visual imagery to inspire creative writing, which then leads on to specific workshops for each of the images contained within the 'Gallery' section; these workshops are optional and are offered only as suggestions, as teachers may choose to incorporate these images into their own teaching methodologies.

This chapter contains a short case study on Michael Morpurgo, detailing how a drawing in Tate Britain inspired his novel *The Last Wolf* (Transworld); the case study features a reproduction of the drawing as well as an extract from the novel and a short interview clip in which Michael discusses how the drawing informed his book.

The 'Music' chapter provides general advice on how music may be introduced in the classroom to initiate creative writing. This section also includes the accompanying compact disc and there are specific activities that relate to each track on the CD. As with the workshops from the 'Images' chapter, these are optional and are offered only as suggestions. The CD features eight tracks in all - three soundscapes and five instrumental pieces. This chapter concludes with an illuminating piece written by Berlie Doherty in which she discusses how music plays a significant role in her own writing, as well as three wonderful pieces of writing - inspired by the first track on the CD - from three young writers at St Andrew's School in Wantage, Oxfordshire.

The word wheels (adapted from an original idea devised by Colin Grigg of the Tate Galleries' Visual Paths programme) that appear towards the end of this book are yet another method of sourcing ideas. These are to be photocopied and assembled either by teachers or by the children themselves. Children can have fun matching together different couplings and deciding which would prove the most interesting starting point for a piece of writing.

Many of the poetry workshops throughout this book encourage young writers to write mainly free verse and not rhyming verse. Rhyme is a seductive tool but can be a stranglehold on the imagination, at a time when young writers should be concentrating on more important issues such as self-expression, imagery, meaning, phrasing, structure and other aspects of language (such as rhythm, alliteration, assonance). There are two examples of free verse in the 'Text and Themes' chapter - Michael Rosen's 'Thirty-Two Lengths' (p. 9) and my own poem 'Night Car Journey' (p. 41). Rosen's poem is colloquial and anecdotal and tells of a childhood experience. My own poem, on the other hand, concentrates on language, and uses alliteration and internal rhyme and gives emphasis to imagery. These can both be used as different models of free verse prior to children writing their own pieces.

Although free verse is closer to speech and thought, children can initially experience difficulties in writing in this form as opposed to rhyming and metrical verse. One way of overcoming this is to display free verse poems on classroom walls so children are used to seeing the format, layout and structure of free verse on a daily basis. Should teachers want to explore the concept of free verse further, I wholly recommend Michael Rosen's book *Did I Hear You Write?*, in which he gives first-hand accounts of working with children in classrooms as a visiting writer and how he approaches his free verse workshops writing autobiographical poems.

Just Imagine recognises and respects that creative writing at all levels is a craft skill that requires the practice, patience and perseverance of any other art form - such as painting, sculpting or playing a musical instrument. Although this book offers many ideas for developing writing in a variety of forms and genres, the primary purpose here is to focus upon the ideas stage - to explore ways of discovering and generating ideas for writing. A variety of texts that deal with other aspects of creative writing is listed in 'Recommended Books' on p. 111.

Every teacher will have his or her own way of running and structuring a creative writing workshop. This outline can easily be modified or adapted:

- freewriting (optional) - in which children write non-stop on any topic for a few minutes - this is to help unlock creativity;
- briefly informing the pupils what they will be writing later;
- discussion of writing activity/reading a text as a model;
- the writing activity (this aspect may well have its own substructure and will depend on the stimuli being used - see the introductions to the 'Images' and 'Music' chapters, if using images or music);
- sharing writing - in partners, small groups or whole class;
- conclusion - where to take the writing next - discussion of developing, revising, drafting and editing;
- publishing - when writing has been edited and drafted.

This book is intended for KS3 and Upper KS2; however, many elements - workshops and stimuli - could easily be modified for use with GCSE and A level, or even adult classes, teacher training classes and creative writing groups. Should teachers wish to comment on any of the materials or workshops in this book, please do write to David Fulton Publishers - your responses would be much appreciated.

*   *   *

Before I conclude with a long list of thank-yous, I wish to explain briefly about one of the photographs in the 'Images' chapter which has aroused some interest. I recently inherited the photograph of the elephant at a circus on p. 69 from my mother. The second gentleman on the ground from the right is my father, and the picture was taken at Billy Smart's Circus (Billy Smart is one of the other horizontal gentlemen) in the early 1960s, and the photograph apparently appeared in a national newspaper at the time.

A number of writers and specialists have inspired and informed some of the philosophies and approaches of this book - namely Celia Rees, Michael Rosen, Michael Morpurgo, Janni Howker and Russell Hoban, as well as Colin Grigg, coordinator of the excellent Visual Paths education project at the Tate Galleries in London. So I wish to thank all of these people. And many thanks also go to those authors that have taken time to write short pieces for various sections in this book - Berlie Doherty, Terry Deary, Pie Corbett, Norman Silver, Jacqueline Wilson, Celia Rees and David Almond.

I wish to thank the English specialist students on the BA Ed. degree at Reading University for being the first 'guinea pigs' with a number of the activities contained here. Specific and special thanks must go to a former BA Ed. student, Donna Livingstone, for suggesting that I incorporate music in my poetry writing workshops; without her suggestion, there would be no music chapter and CD with this book. Thanks must go to my friend and colleague at Reading University, Michael Lockwood, for his ongoing support. Thanks also to the staff of St Andrew's School in Wantage for allowing me to run some writing workshops - as well as to the children for producing such inspiring writing, examples of which are featured in this book.

As ever, much gratitude must go to my editor Helen Fairlie, whose patience, creativity and insight never fails to amaze me. Many thanks also to various other individuals from other publishing houses: Annie Eaton, Kate Giles, Naomi Cooper at Transworld, Nyree Jagger and Hazel Riley at Scholastic, Jo Williamson at HarperCollins; and thanks also to Vicky Ireland, Stephen Midlane and Judith Howard at the amazing Polka Theatre in Wimbledon.

Next, I wish to thank Mark Hawkins, a great friend, an outstanding musician/composer/producer and an unbelievably generous individual. Mark has most kindly donated all of his superb compositions on the accompanying CD free of charge, and has given up much of his valuable time to work on this project. Thanks also to the inimitable Kenny Stone for allowing me to feature his fine track 'Time Piece' on the CD and for his nifty drumming on the piece 'Jangle'. Thanks too to Ken Bentley for the wonderful wedding photo in the 'Images' chapter and for creating the word wheels for me when he should be out doing far more important things such as directing; thanks to Nic and Sue Capon for letting me reproduce the photo of their wedding day in Abingdon. Thanks too to Rob Vincent for his excellent photographs that feature throughout the 'Images' chapter. Many thanks also to two of the very finest contemporary children's illustrators - Ian Beck and Peter Bailey - for their illustrations in the 'Gallery' section; and to Ian Beck for yet another absolutely wonderful cover.

Special thanks must go to Colin Grigg of the Tate Galleries for all his expertise on using images for creative writing, as well as for taking me on a very entertaining and informative tour of Tate Britain. And many, many warm thanks to the following for supporting me with my own creative writing - Jacqueline Wilson, Annie Eaton at Transworld, Brian Moses and Ian Brown. Most of all, I thank my fantastic wife, Sarah, for her unending supply of encouragement, patience and loving support.

With a massive great welcome and infinite love, I dedicate this book to my new friend and daughter, Madeleine Grace Carter, born 30 October 2001.

Acknowledgements

Text and Themes

David Almond - extract from short story 'The Baby' in *Counting Stars* (Hodder Headline). Reproduced by permission of Hodder and Stoughton Ltd.

Enid Blyton - extract from *The Twins at St Clare's* (Mammoth). © Enid Blyton Ltd (a Chorion Company). (All Rights Rerserved.)

James Carter - poem 'Night Car Journey' from *Cars Stars Electric Guitars* (Walker Books).

James Carter - stanza from 'There's Nothing' from *Cars Stars Electric Guitars* (Walker Books).

James Carter - stanza from 'Haiku Triptych' from *Cars Stars Electric Guitars* (Walker Books).

James Carter - stanza from 'Santa: Ace Guy or Strange Bloke?' from *We Three Kings - Christmas Poems*, chosen by Brian Moses (Macmillan).

James Carter - stanza from 'The Charles Darwin Rap' from *Hysterical Historicals: The Victorians*, chosen by Brian Moses (Macmillan).

James Carter - 'Elephant' kenning.

Helen Cresswell - extract from *The Nightwatchmen* (Hodder Children's Books).

Berlie Doherty - extract from *Tough Luck* (Collins Lions).

John Foster - poem 'Four o'clock Friday' from *Four o'clock Friday* (Oxford University Press). © 1991 John Foster, included by permission of the author.

Janni Howker - extract from 'Jakey' from *Badger on the Barge* (Walker Books, 1994).

Vicky Ireland - extract from stageplay of *Kensuke's Kingdom*, adapted from Michael Morpurgo's original novel (Mammoth).

Ian Mcmillan - poem 'Elephant Dreams' from *The Best of Ian Mcmillan* (Macmillan).

Michael Morpurgo - extract from *The Last Wolf* (Doubleday).

Celia Rees - extract from *Witch Child* (Bloomsbury).

Michael Rosen - 'Thirty-Two Lengths' from *Quick, Let's Get Out of Here* (Scholastic Ltd).

Norman Silver - extract from *A Monkey's Wedding* (Faber & Faber).

Alison Uttley - extract from *Traveller in Time* (Puffin). © Alison Uttley 1939, reprinted by kind permission of the trustees of The Alison Uttley Literary Property Trust.

All interview extracts reproduced with the kind permission of the authors: David Almond, Malorie Blackman, Helen Cresswell, Terry Deary, Berlie Doherty, Morris Gleitzman, Brian Moses, Michael Morpurgo, Matthew Sweeney, Jacqueline Wilson and Benjamin Zephaniah - as well as Colin Grigg, co-ordinator of the Visual Paths education programme at Tate Galleries, London.

Images

Peter Bailey - two illustrations: girl with baby/cat funeral from *The Sea Baby* compiled by Susan Dickinson (Collins); illustration of girl and boy in kitchen from *A Chest of Stories for Nine Year Olds* collected by Pat Thomson (Corgi).

Ian Beck - cover illustration; images of 'Mr Nice and Mr Nasty'; insects with flowers.

Ken Bentley - photograph of wedding.

James Carter - photographs of thatched cottage and shoes.

Rob Vincent - photographs of boy on bicycle, boys with boat, London at night, child at table, exit of Tottenham Court Road tube station, car scrapyard.

Bethan Matthews - map of Southridge.

Imperial War Museum - children celebrating VE Day.

Holland House Library, 23 October 1940. Reproduced with permission of English Heritage, NMR.

Various images reproduced by kind permission of Tate Britain, all images © Tate, London 2001:

'An Ancient Castle' by Sir Robert Ker Porter from Oppe Collection at Tate Britain.

'Heads of Six of Hogarth's Servants' by William Hogarth.

'Punch on May Day' by Benjamin Robert Haydon.

'Wolf' by Henri Gaudier-Brzeska.

Music

Ian Andrew, cover from *Midnight Man* © 1998 Ian Andrew. Reproduced by permission of the publisher, Walker Books Ltd, London.

'City Trains' - James Carter/Mark Hawkins.

'Big Bright Moon' - James Carter.

'Time Piece' - Kenny Stone.

'Fisher Boy' - Mark Hawkins.

'Jangle' - James Carter.

'Not So Wicked' - Mark Hawkins.

'War Bird' - Mark Hawkins.

'The Lemming Years' - James Carter.

Contributing authors

The following authors have most kindly contributed interview material to this book:

David Almond (published by Hodder Headline).

Malorie Blackman (published by Transworld, Puffin, Macmillan).

Pie Corbett (published by Macmillan, David Fulton, Oxford University Press).

Helen Cresswell (published by Hodder, Oxford University Press).

Terry Deary (published by Scholastic, Orion, Faber & Faber).

Berlie Doherty (published by Penguin, Hodder Headline, Egmont, Walker Books).

Alan Durant (published by Walker Books, Bodley Head).

John Foster (published by Oxford University Press, Collins).

Morris Gleitzman (published by Puffin, Macmillan).

Tony Mitton (published by Scholastic, David Fickling Books, Orchard, Walker Books).

Michael Morpurgo (published by Transworld, Macmillan, Egmont, HarperCollins).

Brian Moses (published by Macmillan, Hodder Wayland).

Norman Silver (published by Faber & Faber, Hodder).

Matthew Sweeney (published by Faber & Faber).

Jacqueline Wilson (published by Transworld, Puffin).

Benjamin Zephaniah (published by Puffin, Bloomsbury).

Text and **Themes**

'Reading and writing are two sides of the same coin.'
(Matthew Sweeney, poet)

'To be a writer, you've got to be a reader.'
(Alan Durant, novelist)

WRITING WITH TEXT

Ask any author for advice on creative writing, and invariably one of the responses you will receive will be along the lines of 'Read as much and as widely as you can.' As the opening quotes to this chapter remind us, reading and writing are wholly intertwined. For, without having read and enjoyed and loved reading books as children, authors would not be inspired and motivated to go on and write their own poems, stories, plays and novels as adults.

This chapter takes seven common and popular themes from various forms of literature, and uses these as focal points for creative writing. These themes are memories, dreams, school life, friendships, outsiders, journeys and time. Each of these sections contains text examples from fiction to poetry, drama to autobiography, as well as author interview extracts. Each of the text extracts in this section can be photocopied. The blank space on each page with a text extract is intended for brainstorming ideas and notes.

The material that follows can be used directly with a class.

*   *   *

There is a range of pieces in this chapter for you to explore, but you may also wish to discover some poems or extracts from books, plays or short stories for yourself. Once you have chosen a text, read it through a few times, then jot down any initial thoughts, feelings and responses you may have.

Here are some areas that you may wish to think about, write down or even discuss:

*   Why do you like the piece of writing? What do you like about it?
*   Is there anything in the piece that you would like to achieve in your own writing?
*   How does it make you feel/respond as a reader? What effect does it have upon you?
*   Can you relate to or identify with the theme/subject/situation in any way?
*   How would you describe the style of writing?
*   How would you describe the tone/atmosphere?
*   Is it written in the third or first person, and from whose point(s) of view?
*   Is there anything about the language - any words or phrases - that you like?
*   Are there any interesting or unusual metaphors or similes?
*   Does it remind you of another piece of writing - if so, what are the similarities?

GENERAL TEXT ACTIVITIES

1. Once you have chosen a novel or short story, you could use one of these ideas for writing your own story:

- Write another story for the main character(s).
- Write a new story for the central character(s) but in a different time - the future or the past - and/or in a different setting.
- Introduce a new character that interacts with/gets to know the characters from your book.
- Write a sequel or prequel for the book.
- Give the story a different ending.
- Use the same setting but stage another event/scenario there, and introduce all new characters.
- If your book or story is in a set genre - perhaps a thriller, school story or science fiction story - write a new piece in that genre.

2. Find a poem that you like, and use one of these ideas for writing your own poem:

- Borrow the title and write your own poem to it - and once you have written your own poem, you could even think of a new title if you wish.
- Borrow the opening line and write a poem to it - again, you could put in an opening line of your own if you wanted to once you have finished - and remember to state at the bottom where you borrowed the line from.
- Write some new stanzas for a poem you like.
- Write a new poem in the same style, using the same voice, tone and language.
- If your poem is narrated by one character, write another poem in that voice.
- If your poem is in a set form - perhaps a rhyming poem, free verse, haiku or kenning - write a new poem in that form.
- Retell a favourite story in the form of a poem - perhaps a fairy tale, fable, myth or legend - and do not worry about including all of the original details.

3. Find a book that you enjoy and consider ways of adapting it into other literary forms/media:

- Keep a diary for one of the main characters.
- Write a poem as if it was written by one of the main characters.
- Write a monologue in the voice of one of the main characters talking about their life/situation.
- Write a newspaper report on one of the main events in the story.
- Retell the story in the form of a mini-saga - a story told in exactly 50 words.
- Adapt one scene from a book into a TV screenplay: plan it in the form of a story-board, and then into a scene with dialogue.
- Adapt a sequence from a book into a short dramatic scene; pick a moment that is ideally a conversation between a few characters; add extra dialogue of your own; even improvise scenes with friends - first record your improvisations and then do a transcript and develop it further from there if you wish.

- Take a character from a book and create a short film for that person; look for a 'What if . . .' scenario to generate a story for the character - such as 'What if s/he was in danger? . . .' or 'What if s/he was told a secret that was impossible to keep? . . .'.

4. Rework some fairy/folk tales:

- Retell a fairy/folk tale in a different medium - a rap poem, a newspaper report, an exchange of letters or even a few scenes for a pantomime!
- Write a 'What if . . . ?' tale, such as: What if the wolf from 'Little Red Riding Hood' met the giant from 'Jack and the Beanstalk' or the beast from 'Beauty and the Beast'? What would happen if all three met? Or put together other fairy-tale characters. You could write the fairy tale as prose, as a poem, as a short play or as a comic strip.
- Rewrite a fairy tale from the point of view of one character, and in the first person. For example, you could write 'Aladdin' from the genie's point of view, 'Hansel and Gretel' from the father's point of view, 'Cinderella' from one of the two sisters' points of view.
- Pick a minor character from a fairy tale and write their own new story - such as the woodcutter in 'Little Red Riding Hood' or baby bear from 'Goldilocks' say, a few years on.

M E M O R I E S

'What better place to start looking for ideas for your writing than your own memories?'
(Brian Moses, poet)

When we write about our lives - be it in the form of a piece of prose or as a poem or diary - we are doing a number of things. We are celebrating and preserving our memories. We are making sense of and learning from our experiences. We are exploring our feelings. We are comparing the past with the present. We are reliving in our minds and our words what we have done and where we have been - which will help us to make decisions in the future. And, very importantly, we are reminding ourselves of the people who we no longer see or those who are no longer with us.

One piece of advice that children's authors often give to young writers is to keep a diary or journal, as this allows you to write every day, to write privately and at length about the subjects and aspects of your life that matter to you most. Writing a diary or journal is like spreading your thoughts out onto the page, and many people find this a very worthwhile thing to do. What's more, this daily routine is certainly good practice and training for being a professional author. The poet Brian Moses believes that 'Notebooks become treasure chests of memories to dip into and pull out ideas.'

Popular autobiographies in both primary and secondary classrooms in recent years have included such classics as *Boy* by Roald Dahl, *Cider With Rosie* by Laurie Lee, *Zlata's Diary* by Bosnian Zlata Filipovic and *The Diary of Anne Frank*. Unlike these writers, some authors choose not to write autobiographies but to turn their memories into semi-fiction, as David Almond has in his short story collection, *Counting Stars*. In the extract (see p. 7), David Almond tells of a most significant moment in his life. Yet when writing about your memories it is equally important to celebrate the ordinary and everyday moments and events, as Michael Rosen does in many of his autobiographical free verse poems - including the poem that appears here, 'Thirty-Two Lengths'.

DISCUSSION POINTS

- Are your memories important to you? Why?
- Do you enjoy talking about your past? Do you find it useful?
- Are there certain memories that come to you more than others?
- Do you have one or two favourite memories?
- Why do you think that you remember some things and not others?
- Would you like to be able to remember everything in your life? Why?
- What is your earliest memory?
- Do you ever ask any family members about certain moments or events or to tell you about their own lives?

Autobiographical writing

(Related to the extract from 'The Baby' from *Counting Stars* by David Almond.) Spend a while thinking back over your life and find an interesting moment, time or event you could write about. Try to choose something that would be of interest to a reader in some way - perhaps something amusing or significant to you or something important that you want to share with other people. You could pick a small event such as in Michael Rosen's poem 'Thirty-Two Lengths', even a conversation, or something that took place over a period of time, perhaps a series of visits to a place or to see someone.

Autobiographical prose/poem

Write 'I remember' at the top of a sheet of paper and simply start writing about a memory in either prose or as a free verse poem. If you need to stop and make notes because you find that a great many thoughts or ideas come flooding to you or that you want to start all over again with another 'I remember', then that's fine. Alternatively, you could write 'I remember' and then brainstorm a number of memories, and find the one that would make the most interesting piece of writing.

Poem

(Related to Michael Rosen's poem 'Thirty-Two Lengths'.) Think back to a simple moment or event from your life and celebrate it as a free verse poem.

Poem

(Related to the poem 'Night Car Journey' by James Carter in the 'Journeys' section on p. 41.) Read this poem through a few times. Notice how it is written in the present tense, even though the event takes place in the past. This makes the writing more immediate and atmospheric. Choose a special memory of your own. Rather than writing about the entire memory, pick just a few moments. Supposing it was the time you scored a goal; you could describe the few seconds before or after you scored. Or, if it was a holiday, pick just one small aspect of an event from the holiday. Write your own free verse poem in the present tense. Try and use some of the senses if you can - sight (What can you see?), feel (Is it warm or cold?), sound (What can you hear?), and, if relevant, smell and taste. Most of all, tell of the experience as if it was happening to you right now.

Biographical writing/interview

Instead of writing about yourself, you could write about a friend of yours, a school friend, a close or distant relation, a friend of your family or even a neighbour or an older person in your family or community. You could either write about the history of that person's life or pick just one or two events to write about. Or, you could interview that person. Write a list of questions beforehand and take a tape recorder with you to record the interview. Retell the person's story as a biographical piece or as a monologue in the voice of that person.

Fictional autobiography

Write about a fictional character's memories. You could open your piece with one of these sentences:

'I had completely forgotten about it until I heard that song on the radio.'
'I hid the letter in a box under my bed. Until this morning I hadn't read it since I first opened it five years ago . . .'
'Every time I see that photograph I . . .'
'I'm not sure if it's a memory or if I imagined it now . . .'

Diary

Keep a diary for a fictional character that is going through a big change in her/his life. Try to include small, unimportant details as well as the more important ones. The smaller details will help you to build up a full picture of your character and her/his life.

Poem

Think of something important from each year of your life. Write about these in a free verse poem. You could begin each stanza with something like 'When I was one I . . .', 'When I was two I . . .'.

Poem

Write a free verse poem in which you are looking through an imaginary photo album of your life. You could talk about a different photograph/memory in each stanza.

Poem

Write a fun rap poem in which you talk about various aspects of your life or your history. You may want to choose your own beginning or develop your rap from this introduction:

Hey everybody, listen to me -
This is my biography!

Poem

Write about a memory in a syllabic poem such as a haiku, tanka or cinquain (see Glossary - syllabic poetry).

In this extract from 'The Baby' in *Counting Stars* - a collection of short stories by David Almond - the author tells of an important time in his own life:

It was my eleven-plus year. Dad said that I was carrying the dreams of the past, that I was a pioneer. Preparation at school was relentless: day after day of Maths Progress Tests and English Progress Tests and prayers that the hardworking would be rewarded. I took the examination at Jarrow Grammar School. There were scores of us there, ranked and registered in the yard by district and school and name. BAN THE BOMB and great CND symbols were painted on the corrugated roofs of the outside classrooms. Stern teachers stood around us like warders. Even in the toilets we were watched. I stood dazed in there, stared at myself in the cracked mirror, saw the baby and the boy in me, saw the images of my parents upon me. Someone yelled at me to move, to get out. As I stumbled past him he shoved me on my way.

When I began to write in the regimented hall, in a silence broken by scared breathing and the padding feet of invigilators, I began to be released. I knew, as Dad had said, there was nothing for me to worry about, that I would be rewarded.

I passed, and the uniform was grey: grey flannel blazer with a badge of battlements and lances, grey flannel cap, grey shorts and socks. The blazer slopped down over my shoulders, the shorts kept slipping down across my hips. I stood at the centre of the family and they smiled and giggled. Dad put his arm around me and said who knew what wonders time would bring. He took me around the town in his Austin. He burst in on our relatives and called down their congratulations upon me. They laughed at my shyness and pressed coins in my hand. They poured glasses of beer for Dad. His own father told me he'd seen it in me as soon as I was born.

(© David Almond)

Here, David Almond discusses the writing of the book *Counting Stars* - a book that is part-autobiography, part-fiction.

Counting Stars is based on my memories of growing up in a small Tyneside town. It's filled with real people, real places, real events. It's filled with realistic facts. But it's also filled with things I made up - with imaginary facts. This is because, for a writer, reality isn't enough, and sticking to the facts can hold you back from writing interesting stories. In *Counting Stars*, real and imaginary people live side-by side. Real events take place alongside invented events. Real streets lead on to streets that are figments of my imagination. When I wrote these stories, I messed about with the history and geography of my home town. I think it can be a fascinating way to write stories. It can seem difficult and strange at first, but once you begin it's a very enjoyable process. Sometimes you can even forget what you remember and what you made up. It's like creating a whole new world that looks like, but is not, the world you know. It's no longer the familiar, maybe boring place you know so well, but a place that has the ability to surprise and excite you, and a place that you can explore in your stories.

Thirty-Two Lengths
by Michael Rosen
from *Quick, Let's Get Out of Here* (Puffin)

One Tuesday when I was about
ten
I swam thirty-two lengths
which is one mile.
And when I climbed out of the
water
I felt like a big, fat lump of jelly
and my legs were like rubber
and there was this huge man
there
with tremendous muscles all
over him
and I went up to him and said
'I've just swum a mile.'
And he said,
'How many lengths was that
then?'
'Thirty-two,' I said.
And the man looked into the
water and said,
'I've got a lad who
can do ninety.'

D R E A M S

'Sometimes I think dreams are stories trying to come out.'
(Morris Gleitzman, novelist)

Dreams are the brain's way of storing and processing and working through everything that we experience during the day. Nick Arnold, in *Bulging Brains* (Scholastic) tells us that dreams are 'mixed-up memories'. Indeed, dreams are based upon our own experiences and memories, but everything is changed around. More often than not, our dreams do not seem to make any sense at all.

Some say that dreams are a way of telling the future, others say that we dream in opposites. Scientists believe that we only dream for a small portion of the time that we are asleep; it just seems as if we've been dreaming for a longer period.

Dreams and the whole process of dreaming have interested writers since storytelling began and continue to inspire the poets, film-makers, playwrights and novelists of today.

Novelist and screenwriter Malorie Blackman talks about using dreams in the interview extract that follows (p. 16). Some authors even include their characters' dreams in a story, such as in the the extract from Janni Howker's short story 'Jakey' (p. 15); likewise, in the novel *Wolf*, Gillian Cross retells the fairy tale 'Little Red Riding Hood' as an ongoing nightmare that the main character has throughout the book.

DISCUSSION POINTS

- Do you always dream? Do you like dreaming?
- How do you feel about your dreams? Do you think they are important in any way?
- How many of your dreams do you remember?
- Do you remember any dreams from when you were very young?
- Are there certain recurring events or features in your dreams now?
- Have any of your dreams come true?
- Quote from *The Tempest* by William Shakespeare: 'We are such stuff as dreams are made on/and our little life is rounded with a sleep.'

Poem

(Related to Ian Mcmillan's 'Elephant Dreams'.) Create a poem which is divided into a number of short sections of mini-poems. Now write down a few notes about your own dreams. You could even keep a dream diary for a while. Give some of your dreams titles. Be inventive with them - write about events that might happen before or after the aspects you can remember. You could write your mini-poems in the first person - in either rhyme or free verse, whichever you feel is best for your material. You could even include what you think about or how you feel about your dreams.

Poem

(Related to Ian Mcmillan's 'Elephant Dreams'.) Read the poem a few times. Even read it out loud. Now think of an animal or insect or bird that interests you and consider different aspects of its life: Where does it live? What does it eat and how does it catch/obtain its food? Does it live near other creatures? Do other creatures prey on this animal? How would you describe its lifestyle? Make a spider web and write down everything you can think of. You could even do research on the animal too. Now consider the following questions, and add these to your spider web - What does that animal worry about? What does that animal hope or wish for? What might it daydream about?

Now take some of your thoughts and ideas and form them into mini-poems, each based upon a dream that the creature may have. Ian Mcmillan's piece is very imaginative, so try to be creative too when you write your own poem. If you discover that you are writing more about the animal's lifestyle than its dreams, then that's fine.

Poem

(Related to Ian Mcmillan's 'Elephant Dreams'.) Write a kenning (see Glossary at back of book) on another animal. Use your imagination to produce an inventive list of actions and qualities for your chosen animal.

Story

(Related to the extract from 'Jakey' from *Badger on the Barge* by Janni Howker.) Read through the extract a few times. Then:

*   continue this dream in the same style; or
*   write another dream that Steven might have; or
*   try to imagine from the various details in the dream what might be going on in Steven's real life and write a short story about what is happening to him at this time.

Poem

Look up some of the paintings by Salvador Dali that have been inspired by dreams. Write down how you feel about the pictures - do they resemble your own dreams? How would you describe these paintings? If you had to paint one of your own dreams would it look anything like this? Write an experimental poem based on one of Dali's paintings in which you use words and phrases imaginatively to express the weird and unusual qualities of the painting. Try to be really creative - you can even invent words, merge words together, write them backwards or upside down; use a computer to create different s H a p E s if you wish. Like a dream, it does not matter if your poem does not make complete sense. With this piece, experimenting is the most important element.

Free verse poem

See 'Music' chapter - the activity related to the track 'Not So Wicked' on the accompanying CD.

'Cut ups' nonsense poems

This is a game used by novelists, songwriters and poets. You can follow this workshop, or discover your own way of doing 'cut ups'. Pick two poems that you like, two very different poems. Write out the first line of each poem in capital letters onto a sheet of white paper and then cut out each word. Mix and match the words until you make some nonsense phrases. Write out each phrase that you like and use this as a basis for a poem - or make a whole poem with 'cut ups'. Experiment further by using everyday words but removing or adding letters, writing words back to front or changing the order of words.

Art/poem

Dreams take real events and mix them all up. Cut out pictures, photographs, headlines - all sorts of clippings from magazines, newspapers and catalogues - and jumble them all up to form a collage. The more colourful and mixed-up your collage is, the better. Look at your collage for a while and write down a list, or brainstorm around a spider web of everything that comes into your head. Once you have done this, use as many of your thoughts to form either a surreal (which means dream-like) story or a free verse poem.

Story

How many times have you seen people write '. . . and I woke up and it was all a dream' at the end of a story because they didn't know how to finish it? Well, in this activity you will begin with a dream. Your character wakes up and certain events from their dream start to come true. The character realises that s/he has had a series of premonitions, yet has the ability to stop and intervene with various occurrences. Work out a plot outline for your story before you begin writing; perhaps you could plan what happens in the dream(s) first, and then work out if your character will intervene with the real event(s).

Story

In some fantasy stories, it's not the dream that is unusual or weird, but what happens when the character wakes up. In Anne Fine's *Bill's New Frock*, a boy wakes up to discover he has turned into a girl overnight! And in Franz Kafka's *Metamorphosis*, a man wakes up to discover he has turned into an insect! Find a fictional character and write a fantasy story in which s/he wakes up to discover they have changed into something or someone else or has changed in some way.

Non-fiction booklet

Research the subject of dreams - either in books, magazines, or the Internet. Go to your local library and ask for specialist books on the subject. For a start, one book you might try is Nick Arnold's *Bulging Brains*. Collect as much information as you can and then write your own booklet on the subject. Think of creative ways of presenting the information - as with Nick Arnold's book, use quizzes, fact files and even true stories.

Elephant Dreams
by Ian Mcmillan
from *The Best of Ian Mcmillan* (Macmillan)

1   I'm so small
     I can crawl
     under a leaf

     and I can look
     into the world
     from underneath

2   There's a huge grey cloud in the sky.
     It's me.
     I float down on to a sycamore
     tree.
     I burst like a bag and the rain falls
     out.
     I swim in my rain like a huge grey
     trout.

3   My
     long
     trunk
     goes
     round
     the
     world
     twice!

4   I am the last elephant
     and I stare into the sun
     as it falls into the night
     and in the fading light
     I know my race is run.
     I am the last elephant.

5   I can't move.
     People are staring at me.

     I can't move.
     People are walking by.

     I can't move.
     Children are pointing at me.

     I can't move.
     Is this where you go when you die?

Extract from 'Jakey' from *Badger on the Barge* by Janni Howker:

That night he dreamed about Jakey's boat. His mam was in the dream. She and Jakey were sailing over the black water and he was watching them from the shore. He saw old Jakey and his mam smiling and waving. They waved their hats. They shouted and laughed but they were too far out to sea for him to hear them. And then he saw the dark shape following the boat. A great grey shape, like a shark, swimming behind, slowly, secretly. He tried to shout to them. He tried to tell them about the great grey fish which swam behind, but his mam and Jakey were too far away to hear him above the sound of *Rosa's* engine.

Over the black sea came the salt-white mist. He knew that the grey following fish would find Jakey in the mist, and his mam, and they would never hear him shouting. Then, in the dream, the strange boy came walking out of the sea, out of the mist, with a sack on his shoulder. He stood before Steven and began to open his sack to show him what was in it.

Extract from an interview with Malorie Blackman:

With my first short story collection, *Not So Stupid!* I used my dreams as starting points. One or two of the dreams were full stories, and all I had to do was to remember them and write them down. With others, like 'Such are the Times' I had a dream about rain being so acidic it would dissolve the flesh off your body. I used that as a starting point. I thought, 'Okay, what would the rain do to people?' As ever, I was playing a 'What if . . . ?' game. I was thinking about what would happen to the character if *this* happened, and if *that* went wrong, *then* what would she do? - and so on. I'm always trying to escalate events in a story. But with short stories, it's a tighter framework, and there's not so much room to expand your story.

SCHOOL LIFE

'The reason why school is such a popular topic with children
is that it takes up such a huge part of their lives.'
(John Foster, poet)

Schools can be one of the best settings for fiction as there is so much potential for writing about interesting characters and situations - as well as interactions and conflicts between pupils and staff. Indeed, some of the most popular books ever written have been set in schools, such as Charles Dickens' *Hard Times*, Enid Blyton's *Mallory Towers* and *St Clare's* series, Gillian Cross's *Demon Headmaster* books, Allan Ahlberg's *Please Mrs Butler* and *Heard It In the Playground*, and, most recently, J. K. Rowling's *Harry Potter* series.

DISCUSSION POINTS

- If you could change one thing about school, what would it be? Why?
- Do you remember how you felt in your first week at infant school?
- What do you think you will miss most of all about school when you leave?
- What are the three most important things you learn at school? Why?
- What are your thoughts on a) boarding schools b) single-sex schools?
- How do you think schools have changed in the last 100 years?
- How will schools change over the next 100 years?
- Would you make a good teacher?

Story

(Related to the extract from *Tough Luck* by Berlie Doherty.) Read through the extract a few times. Use this as the opening to your own story. You could begin the next paragraph with an event that takes place the next morning, at the beginning of term. Keep your main characters to a maximum of four, if possible. But first read through Berlie Doherty's comments on how she wrote the novel. As with the author, you could invent your characters in groups, and then go on to write your own stories using these characters. You could write the story from the point(s) of view of either the pupils or a teacher.

Story

(Related to the extract from *Tough Luck* by Berlie Doherty.) Read through this opening a few times. Use this as the setting for your own story. Write the story from the point of view of the caretaker - a story in which he tells of an incident that takes place in the playground on the first day of term.

Story

(Related to the extract from *The Twins at St Clare's* by Enid Blyton.) Read through the extract and continue the story. Tell the story of what happens next, but from the point of view of one of the older girls at the school.

Story

Invent your own school. You can borrow certain features from your own school, but in the main, it must be fictional. Invent a headteacher, a few of the staff, and a handful of pupils. Once you have done this, find a story to tell about your school. Perhaps a secret is discovered about one of the teachers or pupils, or perhaps a school play or concert goes wrong. Find the story you want to tell.

Story

Many school stories begin with a newcomer arriving at a school. Think about Harry in the *Harry Potter* series or Dinah in the *Demon Headmaster* series. Invent your own school (see previous activity) and then create a newcomer. Think: What is s/he like? What will the other children think of him/her? Who will they get on/not get on with? In your story, think of what changes will take place because of this new person.

Story

Hogwarts, the school in the *Harry Potter* series by J. K. Rowling, is unusual as it is a school for wizards. Invent your own unusual school - say for witches, aliens, time travellers, circus entertainers, pirates, dragons - and then write a piece about someone's first day at that school.

Story openings

- 'The school in the old house had closed down years ago - well, that's what everyone had said. When Ben and I walked past the other afternoon as it was getting dark, we thought we could see a candle up in the top attic window. I told Ben not to but he . . .'
- 'Mrs Johnson, the class teacher, had hated doing "Show & Tell" ever since Ryan joined her class last term. He brought in the most unusual and unpleasant things. Last week . . .'
- 'The playground fell silent. Nobody said a word . . .'

Monologue

Write a monologue in the voice of a fictional teacher. Perhaps s/he could be talking about what certain pupils get up to in her/his class, what it is like to do break duty, or generally how s/he feels about being a teacher.

Poem

What do you remember about your first few weeks at school? Write about them in a free verse poem in the first person.

Poem

Write a poem - free verse or rhyming - that is a collage of different events taking place in a playground.

Poem

Allan Ahlberg's two poetry collections *Please Mrs Butler* and *Heard It In the Playground* tell of so many different aspects of school life, such as assemblies, registration time, a grumpy teacher, journeys to school, the playground and school projects, to name but a few. Celebrate some school moments, events or routines in either a free verse poem, or a rhyming poem or rap poem or conversation poem. You could even read some of Allan Ahlberg's poems from these two books to see if they inspire ideas of your own.

Extract from *Tough Luck* by Berlie Doherty (Collins):

It's late evening in early January, winter-cold. Mighty-mouth Mulloney, the school caretaker, makes his last rounds of the school before the start of the new term. The corridors are as quiet as ghosts. He glances briefly into the silent rooms to check that chairs and desks are straight, and goes across the yard to the mobiles. The cleaners have left the blackboard as it was at the end of term - *Merry Christmas 3B* chalked across it in bright red, and, hastily sketched in the corner, a green and white bunch of mistletoe and the words *Joe Bead and Miss Peters*, xx. 'Daft twits!' He rubs the board clean and stamps the duster down in its pink chalk-cloud. Then he switches off the light, and pauses for a moment, enjoying the strange peacefulness of the room in the moonlight.

'Circus tomorrow!' he says aloud. 'Roll up! Bring in the clowns!' He locks the door, pulling his coat collar up against the smack of cold. 'And the lion-tamer, heaven help him.'

Banks of dense cloud roll across the moon, and a shiver of sleet like tossed gravel grazes his cheeks. He runs the last few yards to his bungalow.

(© Berlie Doherty)

In this interview extract, Berlie Doherty explains how she wrote the novel *Tough Luck* with the assistance of a class in a secondary school:

My book *Tough Luck* came about when I was doing a writing residency in a school in Doncaster. As soon as I met the Year 8 group I thought, I want to do something sustained with them rather than doing eleven different writing exercises every Wednesday morning. So I said 'Do you fancy writing a book with me?' And they all said 'Yeah!'. We decided the story would be set in a comprehensive school like theirs, a class just like theirs, children just like themselves, but not about them - and that was the most important thing for me to say.

We were going to invent characters who could be in the school. I split the class into groups and each group had responsibility for a character. We drew up character descriptions. I fired questions at each group - such as 'What does he like to eat?', 'What did he dream about last night?', 'What does he wear when he's not wearing school uniform?' Next I gave them scenes to think about.

Therefore there were two books growing at the same time - the one I was writing at home and the school one. By the time I'd finished - which was after the eleven hours of seeing them, there were sixty pages of their book, which they called *Twagger*. We had it reproduced and everyone in the class had a copy. I told my editor Jane Nissen about it and she thought that it was a lovely idea for a new book. And there I was, with a new book to write.

I did a huge amount of research with the ethnic minorities adviser in Sheffield, and going to the Mosque and talking to the Imam at the Mosque. I needed to know more about the character Naseem, as her background was so different from my own. I kept popping back into the school to tell the children how things were developing, to read drafts to them and then we had the launch at the school, which was brilliant.

Edited extract from *The Twins at St Clare's* by Enid Blyton (Mammoth):

Mrs O'Sullivan took the twins to London. They taxied to Paddington Station, and looked for the St Clare train. There it was, drawn up at the platform, labelled St Clare. On the platform were scores of girls, talking excitedly to one another, saying good-bye to their parents, hailing mistresses, and buying bars of chocolate from the tea-wagons.

The twins hugged their mother. 'Good-bye,' said Mrs O' Sullivan. 'Do your best this term, and I do hope you'll be happy at your new school. Write to me soon.'

The twins got into a carriage where three or four other girls were already sitting and chattering. They said nothing, but looked with interest at the scores of girls passing by their compartment to their places further up the train.

At their last school the twins had been the oldest and biggest there - but now they were the youngest! At Redroofs all the girls had looked at Pat and Isabel with awe and admiration - the two wonderful head-girls - but now the twins were looking at others in the same way!

The journey was quite fun. Everyone had packets of sandwiches to eat at half-past twelve, and the train steward brought bottles of ginger-beer and lemonade, and cups of tea. At half-past two the train drew in at a little platform. A big notice said 'Alight here for St Clare's School'.

There were big school-coaches outside and the girls piled themselves in them, chattering and laughing. One of them turned to Pat and Isabel.

'There's the school, look! Up on that hill there!'

FRIENDSHIPS

'Friends are like reflections of yourself.'
(Norman Silver, novelist and poet)

Friendship is a very common and popular theme in all forms of fiction: think of the characters Buzz and Woody in the recent animations *Toy Story* and *Toy Story 2* - and even the theme song 'You've Got a Friend in Me'. Think of the friendships between the characters in soap operas such as *Neighbours* or *Byker Grove* or *Hollyoaks*. In recent novels there have been such friendships as Michael and Mina in David Almond's *Skellig* and Lyra and Will in Philip Pullman's *His Dark Materials*. Often such stories focus upon unlikely friendships - with two characters from very different backgrounds and situations coming together. At first, these two people might not get on, but eventually they will form a long and lasting friendship.

DISCUSSION POINTS

- What are the qualities of a good friendship?
- Are friendships important? If so, why?
- Why are all friendships different?
- Why do some friendships last and not others?
- Are friends as important as relations?
- What is the difference between a friend and a best friend?
- Should you share all your secrets with a best friend?

Drama

(Related to extract from playscript of *Kensuke's Kingdom*, adapted by Vicky Ireland.) Read through the play extract a few times. Write a couple of scenes that take place before this. Take into account the fact that Michael and Kensuke are from very different cultures and generations - what would they talk about or do together on this island? How would they fend for themselves? Alternatively, if you know the story, write about yourself on the island with Kensuke; before you write, think about how you would get on with Kensuke and how you would survive on such an island.

Drama

Write one of these scenes involving two friends (or improvise with someone in your class) in which one says to the other:

- 'Why didn't you tell me about . . .'
- 'I don't know the best way to tell you this, but . . .'

- 'If we're supposed to be friends, how come . . .'
- 'You've changed. You're not the . . .'

Story

There are two people, one old and one young, on a journey together. They do not know each other, and have never met before, they are simply sat next to each other. Eventually, they become very good friends, and one of them will be of great help to the other. Think: Who are they? Are they on a bus, coach, train, plane? Where are they each going to? Why does one of them need help? Write their story in the third person.

Story

A number of recent novels for young people have portrayed friendships between grandfathers and their grandsons - in which they both learn from each other - such as Michael Morpurgo's *Farm Boy*, Norman Silver's *The Blue Horse* and David Almond's *Kit's Wilderness*. Write your own piece, either as prose or as a short drama in which you tell of the friendship between a grandparent and grandchild.

Story

(Related to the extract from *A Monkey's Wedding* by Norman Silver.) Read through the extract a few times. Consider the style, the use of language, and also that one of the characters in the story acts as narrator. Continue this piece and tell of the rescue operation the friends undertake.

Story/Drama

(Related to the extract from *A Monkey's Wedding* by Norman Silver.) Whole-class activity - read through the extract. Now create your own club. The class can be divided into four groups and each will invent a character, a member of the gang. Create a character profile for each one - giving age, physical description, background, likes/dislikes and so on. These four characters belong to a club or gang similar to 'Raisins to the Rescue'. Give the club a name. Now everyone in the class will write their own story - or even a short drama - featuring these four friends. If you want to write a drama, this could be improvised with four members of the class at a time.

Story

Think of all the detective double acts there have been in books and films - Holmes and Watson, Morse and Lewis, Cagney and Lacey, Starsky and Hutch - or even Thomson and Thompson from Herge's *Tintin* books! Create your own detective double act. Perhaps, as with most of these partnerships, you could make your team an unlikely duo - two different personalities that complement each other well. Once you have created your two detectives, think about a case - a murder or robbery perhaps that they could solve. You could write it as a short story or even as a short play. This could even be a comedy, if you wish.

Story

Malorie Blackman's powerful novel *Noughts & Crosses* is, in one respect, a modern-day version of Shakespeare's play *Romeo and Juliet* in that it tells of a forbidden relationship. Write your own story in which two people - of either gender - are for some reason forbidden to see each other by their parents or the community/society that they live in.

Story

An epistolary story is one that is told in letters, e-mails, postcards or faxes - in fact anything that can be sent between two characters. Write your own epistolary story. First, decide who the two characters are. Think - have they ever met? How do they know each other? Why are they writing to each other? How are they writing to each other - e-mails, letters, faxes, text messages etc.? Do a very brief character sketch for each person and then you can begin by one writing to the other. In their communications, the friends will write about ordinary everyday events and thoughts, but try to create a situation that builds over a period of time, perhaps something that is happening in the life of one of the two friends.

Story opening sentence

Pick one of these openings to a story and continue.

* 'It's difficult being really good friends with . . . because s/he's so extraordinary. I've never known anyone quite like her/him. I mean, have you met anyone that . . .'
* 'It would be true to say that we didn't like each other when we first met, but now . . .'

Poem

Write a free verse poem in which you celebrate a special time or occasion that you spent with a close friend(s). Perhaps it will be about someone who you no longer see.

Michael Morpurgo's novel *Kensuke's Kingdom* tells the story of Michael, a young English boy, who is marooned with his dog, Stella, on an island in the Pacific Ocean, having fallen overboard from his parents' yacht. Michael eventually befriends an old Japanese man living on the island who calls him 'Micasan'. The two form a very special bond, and Kensuke becomes a surrogate father for the boy. Below is an edited extract which is taken from Vicky Ireland's stage adaptation, in which the two notice a yacht out at sea:

[They are painting in a cave.]

Kensuke: [Looking at what Michael has done.] Very fine pictures, Micasan. [Stretching.] I go for walk. [He walks out of cave, stretches, sees something out at sea. He breathes and points with stick.] Micasan. The binoculars, and bring fire, quick!

[Michael brings binoculars and lighted stick.]

Michael: A sail. Two sails!! It's a yacht!!

Kensuke: Yes. Yes. It's a boat. Light beacon, Micasan.

[They go to beacon. Michael lights it.]

Michael: The yacht's not turning. Why doesn't this fire smoke?

Kensuke: Do not worry. They see this for sure, you see.

[They take turns with the binoculars.]

Michael: [Getting desperate.] It's still not turning.

[They throw on more wood.]

Kensuke: Micasan, it is coming. I think the boat is coming.

[He hands the binoculars to Michael.]

Michael: It's turning, but which way, towards us or away?

Kensuke: I tell you Micasan, it come this way. They see us. I am very sure. It come to our island.

[They hug each other. Michael leaps up and down with joy and Stella barks. We see already Kensuke's sadness.]

Kensuke: You listen to me very good now, Micasan. I am too old for that new world you tell me about. It is very exciting, but it is not my world.

Michael: But -

The following piece is an edited extract taken from the novel *A Monkey's Wedding* (Faber & Faber) by Norman Silver. The book is set in Johannesburg, South Africa and tells the story of four teenage girls, who are close friends yet come from different backgrounds.

Even then, Rebecca was a leader. She was always the one with the ideas that drove what we did each day. She'd think up things to do, places to go, pranks to play on people. She was inventive and I found it so exciting just to be with her. And Jay and Thuli felt just as I did.

One of the earliest things Rebecca invented for us was a club. She called us 'Raisins to the Rescue', because of the advert which said that raisins give you power. At the top of Jay's block of flats we made our den out of cardboard boxes, old chairs, and a piece of corrugated metal that we found. It was our shelter, our hide-out, and we used to eat our raisins in there, jumping around to show how powerful we were. We thought we'd be detectives of the next generation and we'd solve mysteries and crimes. Of course, Rebecca was our chief detective and she sent us on various errands.

One day she sent me and Jay around to this boy's flat. He had a habit of pulling girls' hair at school and we had to put a note under his door that Rebecca had written. It said: 'You are a bully, Trevor, and if you don't stop we are going to tell the police.' The note was signed 'Raisins to the Rescue.' Actually, Rebecca had wanted to capture Trevor and give him a taste of his own medicine, but Thuli stepped in, as she often did when Rebecca's ideas got out of hand, and suggested sending the note instead.

Sometimes we patrolled the park near us. Four detectives on the look-out for misdemeanours. But I think the only crime we ever discovered was someone throwing her crisp packet on the ground. We jumped at the opportunity and told her sternly to pick it up and throw it in the dustbin, but she just walked off laughing at us.

However, Raisins to the Rescue did once carry out a rescue operation.

(© Norman Silver)

Here, Norman Silver talks about the theme of friendship in his books:

Friendships are an exploration of who you want to be. Friends are like reflections of yourself. As you change, how you view your friends can change. A person chooses friends. No one chooses relations - they are given, whether one likes them or not. Friends are allies in the battle to achieve goals. I was excited in *Monkey's Wedding* to write about multi-cultural friendships which would have been impossible in the old racist South Africa - and also to reveal character development through the reactions of this group of friends to challenges and dangers. Their friendship began when they were young with the 'Raisins to the Rescue' club, was consolidated when the girls took an oath to care for each other like sisters, survived tests of loyalty and courage, produced positive and tangible results for each girl and for the community they lived in, yet disintegrated by the end of the novel. The girls go their separate ways having matured and found their own, unique paths in life.

OUTSIDERS

'In my books I tend to focus on the child that's the odd one out,
the child that doesn't fit in for whatever reason, the outsider.'
(Jacqueline Wilson)

The outsider has always been a popular figure. Think of these characters and why they are outsiders: Buzz Lightyear in the original *Toy Story* film, Mowgli in the Disney film of *The Jungle Book*, Alice in Lewis Carroll's *Alice in Wonderland* or even Harry Potter in the first book of the *Harry Potter* series. As a rule, outsiders in stories have a big impact upon the place, community or society or world that they enter, and many changes can occur because of their arrival.

People can be outsiders for all sorts of reasons - whether a bully or a victim (see John Foster's poem on p. 48), someone new to a school, a loner, an individual, someone who is slightly different from everyone else - someone who just doesn't fit in to a place, for whatever reason.

DISCUSSION POINTS

- Have you ever been an outsider?
- Do you feel like an outsider at the moment?
- How does it feel to be an outsider?
- How are outsiders generally treated?
- Have you known an outsider recently?
- Are outsiders treated fairly?

Story

(Related to extract from *The Adventures of Tom Sawyer* by Mark Twain.) Even if you know the story of Huckleberry Finn, write a new adventure for Huck and Tom Sawyer, in which, as always, they end up getting into trouble! Before you start, you might want to do some planning as well as think about what life in those times - in America, and in a small town by the Mississippi River - would have been like.

Monologue

(Related to extract from *The Nightwatchmen* by Helen Cresswell.) Read through the extract and write a monologue in the voice of Josh, the tramp described in this passage. Josh need not tell a story in your monologue, perhaps simply talk about his life and the way that other people treat him and his brother Caleb.

Poem

(Related to extract from *The Nightwatchmen* by Helen Cresswell.) Read through the extract and then write a free verse poem that details a day in the life of one of these two tramp figures, Josh and Caleb. Think about where they may sleep, where they go, what they eat, what they do during the day and what encounters they may have with other people.

Poem

Write a poem from the point of view of a new person starting at school. Begin each stanza with 'On the first day . . .', 'On the second day . . . ' and so on.

Poem

Sometimes poets have a title before they write a poem. Choose one of the following and write either a rhyming or free verse poem: 'New Baby', 'The Stranger', 'The Visitor', 'Odd-One Out'.

Story scenarios

Choose one of these scenarios. Before you begin writing, ask yourself a series of questions - Who is this person? Why are they there? What will happen next?

- Someone walks into a room of strangers.
- Someone wakes up in a strange place.
- Someone turns up on the door step and things change for ever.
- A crime is committed. An outsider is blamed. But who is guilty?

Story

An animal - perhaps a pet, or a wild animal - arrives somewhere for the first time and has a big impact upon the house/family/people/place/community or town. Tell the story from the animal's point of view.

Story

Somebody new arrives into a family - perhaps a new baby, a long-lost member of the family or an adopted brother or sister. Write about one of these from the point of view of one of the existing family members.

Story

A new girl/boy arrives in your class. S/he has only been in the country for a short while. Her/his family had no choice but to leave their own country. S/he speaks a little

English. Tell her/his story from your point of view, and recount how the family fled from their country and are struggling to settle in this country.

Story openings

Write your own outsider story using one of these introductions:

* It all began the day I met . . .
* Things haven't been the same since . . .
* S/he was unlike anyone else I've ever met. For a start . . .

Fairy tale

Take two outsiders from two different fairy tales and write a new fairy tale that tells of what happens when they meet. You could choose from these characters - Snow White, Goldilocks, Rumplestiltskin, the wolf from 'Little Red Riding Hood' - or think of some of your own. If other fairy-tale characters appear in your tale as you write, then that's fine.

Drama

Shakespeare's play *A Midsummer Night's Dream* tells of what happens when a group of people enter an enchanted forest - so humans are the outsiders. The forest is inhabited by magic spirits that cast spells and play tricks upon the unsuspecting group of people. In groups of eight or ten, improvise your own drama - in which half the group are people, the other half are magic spirits. Discuss who your characters are going to be beforehand, and give them names and personalities. Once you have done your improvisation, write your own piece - either a story, poem or short drama script - based upon your own drama; you can by all means add any details of your own.

This passage is taken from a novel written in 1876 and is set in a town by the Mississippi River in America, where the outsider is a boy who is very much a law unto himself (edited extract from *The Adventures of Tom Sawyer* by Mark Twain):

Shortly Tom came upon Huckleberry Finn, son of the town drunkard. Huckleberry was hated and dreaded by all the mothers of the town because he was idle, and lawless, and vulgar, and bad - and because all their children admired him so, and delighted in his forbidden society, and wished they dared to be like him. Tom was like the rest of the respectable boys in that he envied Huckleberry his outcast position, and was under strict orders not to play with him. So he played with him every time he got a chance. Huckleberry was always dressed in his cast-off clothes of full-grown men. He came and went at his own free will. He slept on doorsteps in fine weather, and in empty hogsheads in wet; he did not have to go to school or to church, or call any being master, or obey anybody; he could go fishing or swimming when and where he chose, and stay as long as it suited him; nobody forbade him to fight; he could sit up as late as he pleased; he was always the first boy that went barefoot in the spring and the last to resume leather in the fall; he never had to wash, nor put on clean clothes; he could swear wonderfully. In a word, everything that goes to make life precious, that boy had. So thought every harassed, hampered, respectable boy in St Petersburg. Tom hailed the outcast:
    'Hello Huckleberry!'
    'Hello yourself, and see how you like it.'
    'What's that you got?'
    'Dead cat.'

In this piece - an edited extract from *The Nightwatchmen* by Helen Cresswell (Hodder Modern Classics) - a boy named Henry meets two unusual tramps, brothers Josh and Caleb, in a park one morning:

Henry stared at him as he ate. Dew dangled from the rim of his battered felt hat. The edges of his overcoat were frayed almost to fringes and it was tied round the middle with a rope. His boots were huge and craggy and pieces of sack were tied round his legs like gaiters. It could not have been his clothes that made Henry think, for a moment, of a parson. It was his whiskers, he decided, grey and overgrown. Or it was the wild tufts of eyebrows, or his voice, rich and with built-in echoes as if it were in church.

Abruptly he stuffed the empty bag in his pocket, got up, and began to stamp. His arms flapped across his chest and he roared with the gusto of a furnace bellows.

'Ah! That's better! Get the blood bouncing. Stamp your feet and clap your wings. 'Ello, 'ere's Caleb.'

Caleb was pushing his handbarrow towards them between the dripping laurels. The sun flashed on his fiery hair and beard. He was small and neat as a weasel, lard-faced and slippery-looking.

'Not so draughty here as where I been,' he remarked, dropping the handles of his barrow. 'Who's this?'

He stared at Henry.

'Young feller,' explained Josh, 'by the name of . . . ?'

'Henry," said Henry.

'What does he want?' asked Caleb.

Josh shook his head.

'What do you want?' he asked Henry.

In many of Jacqueline Wilson's books there are outsider figures, such as Andy in *The Suitcase Kid* and Tracy Beaker in *The Story of Tracy Beaker* and *The Dare Game*. In this interview extract, Jacqueline explains why she is interested in writing about outsiders:

In my books I tend to focus on the child that's the odd-one out, the child that doesn't fit in for whatever reason, the outsider. I suppose I was an odd one out myself. I had lots of friends at school because I learnt at an early age to be reasonably sociable and get on with people and to *pretend* - if I said what I really thought the other kids might feel I was a bit weird. I wanted people to like me so I tried hard to play the sort of games *they* liked, even though they weren't my type of thing at all. I always wanted to play imaginary games. I did find a few friends who liked playing these sort of games too, but mostly I made up all sorts of things by myself, in my own head. I write about children who are very similar!

JOURNEYS

'All my books are like journeys or explorations.'
(Helen Cresswell)

Some of the oldest known stories feature journeys. Over the last 3,000 years, journeys have served as the basis for some of the most famous and popular stories, including Chaucer's *The Canterbury Tales* from the fourteenth century, Jonathan Swift's *Gulliver's Travels* from the eighteenth century and Robert Louis Stevenson's *Treasure Island* from the nineteenth century, J. R. R. Tolkein's *The Hobbit* from the twentieth century, and now at the start of the twenty-first century, Philip Pullman's award-winning trilogy, *His Dark Materials*.

People go on journeys for all kinds of reasons - to escape or avoid a situation, to have time alone, to find something, to go on a quest, to experience new things or other cultures, to visit someone, to meet old friends or relations, to go on holiday or even to go to war. What is useful about writing about a journey is that it gives you a good structure for a story - as you will automatically have a beginning, a middle and an end. There are many fairy tales, where characters, as a result of going on a journey, will gain experience, will learn about themselves and the world, and will mature or become a better or wiser person.

Yet journeys are not only about people travelling from one place to another - journeys can be about individuals growing and developing as people. The author Norman Silver says that his books are about 'children journeying to find themselves'. And in the quote above, Helen Cresswell comments that writing a book is itself like a journey, as it is a process of discovery.

DISCUSSION POINTS

- Where would you like to travel to? Why?
- What is the furthest you have ever travelled?
- What do you like/dislike about travelling?
- Have you or your family been on long journeys?
- Where do your family or ancestors come from? Did they travel great distances?
- What books have you read that feature journeys?

Story

(Related to extract from *Witch Child* by Celia Rees.) Continue the story from here. Imagine what might happen to Mary and Martha both during their journey and when they arrive in America. Consider - why are they travelling to America? Who might they encounter on the ship and on land? And what would America have been like in the year 1659? Try to answer some of these questions before you begin writing.

Story

(Related to extract from *Witch Child* by Celia Rees.) Reset this story of Mary and Martha in the present day. Think: if they were going to America, how would they travel now? - by ship or plane? Write about the start of the journey in the voice of Mary, and express their excitement and nerves about the journey ahead. Use some descriptive phrases - as the author has here - to give your reader some idea of what it is like to be in that place; note how the author concentrates on smell, touch and sound to evoke atmosphere. Also think - why are Mary and Martha going to America? - are they running from or to something? What will happen to them when they get there?

Poem

(Related to the poem 'Night Car Journey' by James Carter.) Read through this poem a few times and see how it captures the mood of a journey at night by car. Think of a small moment from a journey that you have made - perhaps staring out of a train or bus window, a conversation during a journey by car, or even your journey to school. Create your own first-person free verse poem. Write it in such a way that it captures how it feels to be there travelling at that time. You could use some of the senses, writing about what you can see, hear or touch.

Story

Helen Cresswell compares writing a story to a journey: 'With most of my books I simply write a title and a sentence and I set off and the road leads to where it finishes. All my books are like journeys or explorations. When I start on my books - I really don't know what's going to happen, it's quite dangerous, in a way. I often put off starting because it seems a bit scary. Yet at the end of the day, I feel that a story has gone where it's meant to have gone.' For once, do not work out a story plan. Write the title 'The Journey' at the top of your page (you can change it later to what suits your story best) and simply start writing. If, after a while, you want to change your introduction, write down some notes on the story or characters, or even start again, then do so.

Travel writing

Think back to a special journey you have made - it does not have to be abroad, it can even be somewhere close to home. In either a poem or a piece of prose, capture what it was like to be on that journey. Think - who were you with? How did you feel - excited, anxious? - and why did you feel like this? What was it like to be there - in the car, coach, train or on a walk? Include dialogue - conversations with people - to bring the piece to life. Evoke in your words the atmosphere of the place and the sensation of travelling - using sounds, smells and textures, all the different senses that you can. If you want to make your writing lively and vital, you could write in the present continuous tense, for example - 'We are all sitting on a train, going to see grandma at the coast. We are eating our picnic and listening to . . .'

Story

Trains can make great settings for novels, films and plays. Write a piece of your own, perhaps in a set genre, such as a ghost or supernatural story or a mystery story or crime thriller (See 'Genres and Places' word wheel, p. 104). Bring the location to life for your reader - capture all the sounds and the rhythms of a train, let your reader know how it feels to be there. Try to work out a basic plot for your story before you begin. Alternatively, find a picture of a character(s) from the 'Gallery' section of the 'Images' chapter, and send that person (or those people) on a train journey.

Story

Some of the most fascinating stories from the twentieth century are about journeys undertaken on unusual modes of transport. The film *The Straight Story* tells the true tale of an old American man who travelled over 200 miles to see his brother on a lawn mower! The short story 'The Swimmer' by John Cleever tells of a man who swims in all the swimming pools on the journey back to his home. In *Around Ireland With a Fridge*, by Tony Hawks, the author tells of his true journey in which he pulled a fridge around Ireland! Write your own fictional story - perhaps in diary format, or in a series of letters/postcards in which you report a character undertaking an unusual journey, such as swimming from the estuary of a river up to its source or travelling by scooter from Cornwall to London.

Story

Many books about journeys have their hero/heroine face a series of mini-episodes, either difficulties to overcome or encounters with strangers or situations. Write your own journey story in which your hero/heroine has a number of obstacles to overcome.

Film plot/storyboard

'Road movies' are films that are about characters going on long journeys, by car, or in some cases, coach or bus or even hitchhiking. Write your own story for a road movie. It can be set in any country. You could, if you want, have two characters - one child or teenager, and the other an adult - travelling together on the road. Consider: Where are they going? Why? How long will it take them? What problems will they encounter along the way? Is anyone trying to stop them? What will they do when they reach their destination? Do they know exactly where they are going? Are they escaping? Searching for something? Running away from someone or something? However, you may decide to have just one character, but still ask yourself the questions above. Work out a plot first - write down in a paragraph or two where the character will go and what s/he will do.

Fairy-tale journey

Think of the journeys that fairy-tale characters undertake. Both Little Red Riding Hood and Hansel and Gretel journey through the woods. Using one of these characters, change their journey so that they meet up with other characters from fairy tales. First, brainstorm as many characters or character types from fairy tales as you can think of; here are a few to start you off: giants, witches, dwarfs, royalty, talking animals and so on.

Openings

*   'I've never kept a diary before, and I've never been on a journey like this before, so here goes . . .'
*   'S/he took the suitcase down from the top of the wardrobe, piled in as many clothes as s/he could and left the . . .'
*   'I'm going to tell you about this journey I made 50 years ago. You might not believe all of it, but by the end you'll . . .'

Story scenarios

*   Someone arrives somewhere after a long and arduous journey.
*   Someone arrives home after a long journey to discover that a great deal has changed.
*   As someone begins their journey, things don't turn out as expected.

Story

(Small-group activity.) One traditional form of fiction is one in which a group of characters are on a journey together, and to pass the time each tells a story, be it fiction or something from their own experience. In a small group, invent your own group of characters, and think of what journey they might be making together. There are many possibilities, such as explorers in a ship travelling to the Antarctic; astronauts in a space shuttle; a group of strangers that start talking on a long coach journey; a gang of thieves that have smuggled themselves onto a goods train.

Story

Michael Morpurgo's novel *Dear Olly* follows the flight of a migrating bird from England to Africa. Write a story/poem in reverse - a migrating bird coming to England for our summer. Write the story/poem from the bird's point of view and include descriptions of the landscapes it passes over *en route.*

Writing on the move/location

Poets have held writing workshops in all kinds of places, from castle ruins to football grounds, from oil rigs to museums, from art galleries to trains travelling through the mountains in Switzerland. This proves that poems can happen anywhere at any time. Writing in places outside of the classroom can often produce surprising results from pupils. Such poems that begin life in these locations are completed in the classroom. Children bring along pens and paper and make notes or observations and brainstorm ideas. When writing about specific places for example, pupils can be encouraged to use all of their senses - sight, hearing, smell, touch and taste, if relevant. Likewise, metaphors and similes can be used to colour their writing, for example, by encouraging imaginative and metaphorical ways to describe the sound of traffic, a building site, the appearance of a hill or the sky. If the location has a specific historical value or significance, the group can write letters from the point of view of someone who lived in/worked in/passed through this location.

Soundscape

Listen to the soundscape 'City Trains' on the accompanying CD and read the related activities in the 'Music' chapter.

Celia Rees's novel *Witch Child* is set in the year 1659. In this edited extract, the central character is a girl, Mary, and she is travelling with a woman, Martha, to America by ship:

I had never been on a ship before, never seen the sea until a day or so ago. To me, the vessels looked huge. Our ship, the *Annabel*, seemed to stretch nearly the length of a street. It smelt of tar and new wood. As I stepped on board, I felt the subtle rocking motion beneath my feet. I clung to thick rope held taut and creaking by the masts and spars high above me. I was no longer on solid ground.

After our prayers were over, we were directed below to the great cabin. This is to be our home. It seemed a great expanse at first, running nearly from one end of the ship to the other, but it has soon filled up until each person's space is but a bed width.

The sailors sweated and chanted above us, hauling sail and heaving up the great iron chain of the anchor, and we set ourselves up in little groups, piling and positioning our belongings to make enclosures.

'Packed as tight as the cattle in the hold,' I remarked as we arranged our bundles.

'And likely to smell as rank,' Martha nodded towards the slop buckets in the corner. 'Here, strew this in your bedding. I plucked it from my garden just before I left.'

She reached in her pack and handed me a bundle of herbs: lavender and rosemary, fresh and pungent, and meadowsweet dried from another season. The scent took me straight to my grandmother's garden and my eyes blurred with tears. Martha went to speak, but her voice was drowned by a fresh flurry of shouting from above us. The heavy mooring rope fell with a dull thud to the side of the ship. The movement changed, rising and falling in sudden surges of motion. The mainsail cracked as the wind caught it and the whole ship veered, causing people to stagger. We were away.

(© Celia Rees)

This short free verse poem is about the sensation of travelling at night:

Night Car Journay
by James Carter

I wake up
sitting in the back seat
not quite sure
if it's real or a dream

and I look up
out through the darkness
out through the silence
to an infinite sky

and the moon bobs
in and out of treetops
turning the world
a ghostly blue

and my eyes
are heavy now
my eyes
are heavy now
my

(© James Carter)

In a number of Michael Morpurgo's novels the characters undertake long journeys - such as the family in *Kensuke's Kingdom*, the swallow in *Dear Olly*, the soldier in *Billy the Kid* and the children in *Waiting for Anya*. In this interview extract, Michael Morpurgo explains why he has always been fascinated by journeys:

Why do I write about journeys in my books? I think this goes back to my reading as a child, and especially Robert Louis Stevenson. In Stevenson's *Kidnapped* there's a map at the front of the book, and you could follow where the character goes across the mountains and the glens. I loved the constant sense of movement in Stevenson's books, all the different landscapes - from the city of Edinburgh to the mountains and the seas. In *Treasure Island* too, there's also a terrific sense of place and motion. This business of movement has become very important to me as a writer too. I don't particularly like books that are static. I think it's deep within me that books are about journeys, about physical movement from place to place. Yet they're also about moving forwards in our lives, about gaining wisdom and about learning from our experiences. So the physical journey is a metaphor for the spiritual journey that goes on inside us.

TIME

'Everything and everyone moves through time.'
(Terry Deary, author of the *Horrible Histories* series)

The passing of time interests all of us at one point or another in our lives. It may seem obvious to say that time passes in all stories, but only some stories actually have time as a central theme. When we are young we often feel that our lives will stretch out for ever, yet the older we get, the more we give thought to how little time we have, and this is perhaps why so many adult authors write about this topic, as it is something that concerns them in their daily lives.

Time travel was a popular theme in some of the novels of the twentieth century, such as the much-loved classics *The Time Machine* by H. G. Wells and *Tom's Midnight Garden* by Philippa Pearce. Many poems and songs too have been written about the subject of time, and one particular aspect that has concerned poets and songwriters is the subject of ageing and of youth wasting their time and their lives.

DISCUSSION POINTS

- How often do you think about time or the future or the past?
- What ambitions do you have for the future?
- Do you believe time travel will ever be possible?
- Do you think older people perceive time differently from younger people?
- If you could, how would you change the seven days of the week?
- How often do you look at the clock/your watch?
- How do you think you will change over time?
- What shape is time? How would you draw it?
- Think of all the devices we have - new and old - for measuring time.
- Is time important? Why?

Story

(Related to extract from *A Traveller in Time* by Alison Uttley.) Read through this piece a few times. Note how the narrator talks about the sensation of travelling through time, but does not talk specifically about where s/he went. Continue this piece and choose what time the traveller returned to. Consider: Who is Jude? What is this place called Thackers? Also, concentrate on the author's style of writing - her use of words and language and her phrasing - and see if you can adopt some of this in your own writing.

Poem

(Related to the poem 'Four o'clock Friday' by John Foster.) Poems such as this one take the days of the week as a structure. Write your own free verse poem in which every line of each verse or stanza refers to each of the seven days, for example: perhaps the poem tells of your daily routines or even tells a story that begins on a Monday and concludes on either a Friday or a Sunday.

Poem

(Related to poem 'Four o'clock Friday' by John Foster.) Instead of the days of the week, use another time frame for a free verse poem. For example, you could follow the events of a day and begin each stanza with set times from one day - say 7.30 a.m., then 9 a.m., then 10.30 a.m. as different events take place. Or, follow the months of the year, or even the years in a decade - such as 1990, then 1991, then 1992, and so on.

Poem

(Related to poem 'Four o'clock Friday' by John Foster.) Write a free verse poem about bullying at school, in which you use the days of the week as a structure, for example:

> It's Monday morning
> and s/he is dreading going back
> to that playground
> as . . .

Story

Imagine that your class is visiting the Science Musem in London on a school trip. You notice an exhibit with a machine that looks similar to a photo-booth callled 'The Time Machine'. No one is looking, so you enter the machine. There is a screen and keyboard in front of you. The screen asks 'Where do you live?' You type in your address. The screen now asks 'The year 3000 or the year 1000?'. You decide which one you type in. Write about what happens next.

Story

Imagine that you nod off during a class and wake up in a classroom 100 years in the future. Write about your experiences in a piece in the first person. Try to include some passages in which you describe such details as the future school, the classroom and the uniform.

Story

In a fantasy story, write about someone who discovers how to make time stand still. What will this enable this person to do? How will s/he use it to their advantage?

Story

Think of an event in history that you would like to change. What if you were able to go back to that time and change the course of events? Write the story of your experiences in a piece in the first person. Begin at the point when you arrive in the past.

Short drama

In Tony Mitton's poem 'The Child from the Future' (from the collection *Plum*, Scholastic) the narrator of the poem meets up with a young child from the future. The child tells the narrator what a better world we have now. Either write on your own or improvise with a friend a short drama in which you meet up with someone from 500 years into the future. What would you want to ask them? What would they want to ask of you? How will this meeting change your view of the present?

Song lyric

The song 'Time' by Pink Floyd - from the album *The Dark Side of the Moon* - begins with the sound of many alarm clocks going off. There is also the ticking of a clock throughout the song that acts as a rhythm. Imagine a slow, steady ticking beat in your head as you write your own brand-new rap, song lyric or poem with the title 'Time'. If, having written the piece, you decide that there is another and more suitable title, do use it. You could even record your piece onto cassette tape using a ticking clock or metronome as your backing rhythm.

Time capsule

A time capsule is a box or container that holds a number of items, such as newspapers, photographs and everyday objects that someone may discover in the future and will help them to learn about our time. Imagine what you would include in your own time capsule. Now write a letter to the person that will find your time capsule, say in 200 years from now. Divide your letter into two halves: in the first half discuss what life is like now - including your own life - and then move on to what you imagine life will be like in the future. And what objects from now would you include in the capsule? In your letter you could even ask the person who discovers the time capsule a number of questions. You could even develop this by writing a piece in which someone in the year 2200 finds the capsule. What would they make and understand of your letter and the objects inside?

Research/diary

Do some research into your local area, and discover what interesting history it may have. Did the Romans or Stone Age or Iron Age people live in your area? Did a battle take place nearby? Now imagine and write about what it would be like to walk around your area as if it were that time. Write it as if it were a diary entry.

'What if . . .' drama

In her novel *Thief!* (Transworld) Malorie Blackman wrote about a girl who goes into the future and meets herself. Write a small scene - in dialogue - in which you go into the future and you meet the 40-year-old version of yourself. What will the two different ages of you want to ask each other? What will you both want to know? Don't worry about doing a plan, simply start writing.

Time travel openings

- 'Nobody wore clothes like that anymore. And what was he doing out on that hilltop? S/he wanted to run all the way back up again and see if . . .'
- 'S/he knew it was a local myth but that didn't stop her/him coming back to the same spot on midsummer's day at midnight and waiting until . . .'
- 'S/he picked her/himself off the ground and s/he saw that her/his watch had smashed - but more than that, it wasn't morning anymore, it was evening, and where had that house come from? - that was an empty field before . . .'
- 'The numbers on her/his digital watch were actually moving. The digits were moving forwards, faster and faster. They now read 4 p.m., now 5 p.m. until . . .'

A number of novels and short stories from the twentieth century have time and time travel as their major themes, as with Alison Uttley's *A Traveller in Time* (Puffin, 1939):

. . . I had been away for hours, days it seemed, but the fingers of the grandfather clock had not moved while I was away. Like a dream which abolishes time and space, which can travel through years in a flash and to the ends of the world in a twinkling, I went into another century and lived there and returned before the pendulum of the grandfather clock had wagged once behind the bull's eye-glass. I had experienced the delights and anxieties of another age, moving quietly in that life, walking in the garden, talking and loitering and returning in the blink of an eyelid. It was neither dream nor sleep, this journey I had taken, but a voyage backward through the ether. Perhaps I had died in that atom of time, and my ghost had fled down the years, recognised only by Jude, and then returned in a heartbeat . . . I was living in the past and present together, at Thackers, the home of my ancestors. I saw the web and woof of time threaded in a pattern, and I moved through the woven stuff with the silent footfall of a ghost.

(© Alison Uttley)

The following piece is a rhyming poem by John Foster and tells of someone who is precoccupied with time for a very unfortunate reason.

Four o'clock Friday
by John Foster

Four o'clock Friday, I'm home at last,
Time to forget the week that's past.
On Monday, in break they stole my ball
And threw it over the playground wall.
On Tuesday afternoon, in games
They threw mud at me and called me names.
On Wednesday, they trampled my books on the floor,
So Miss kept me in because I swore.
On Thursday, they laughed after the test
'Cause my marks were lower than the rest.
Four o'clock Friday, at last I'm free,
For two whole days they can't get at me.

(© John Foster)

Here, Terry Deary, author of many books, including the popular *Horrible Histories* series (Scholastic) - with such titles as *The Rotten Romans*, *The Vile Victorians*, *Wicked Words* and *The Savage Stone Age* - discusses why he is interested in the concept of time:

Everything and everyone moves through time. The key to a good story is that the central character 'changes' through time. Some historical and fictional characters have been changed through a single, dramatic incident - with Victoria it was the death of her Albert, and with Macbeth it was meeting the witches. Some characters have changed slowly - Henry VIII's rage growing over 30 years of frustration, David Copperfield's childhood-to-manhood learning about overcoming disappointments. The most important character of all - the reader - changes too. Reading about historical and fictional characters helps the reader understand human change. So, stories can help the reader manage the changes that will happen in their own lives. Forget dramatic plots and action, forget vivid descriptions of places. Concentrate on changes in human behaviour over time. Everything and everyone moves through time - other people's stories can make our own progress through time that much more happy and fulfilled.

Images

'A richness of language and ideas derives from using art as a stimulus
rather than simply using the imagination.'
(Colin Grigg, Visual Paths Coordinator, Tate Galleries)

'I collect images to use as reference. I keep them in front of me
while I'm writing, so that when I look at them, memory and imagination combine
and from that I can re-create the very fabric of a place down to the finest detail.'
(Celia Rees, novelist)

WRITING WITH IMAGES

Images are like frozen moments from narratives. As we view images they arouse our curiosity and can lead us to consider what is taking place and to imagine such things as who the characters in the picture are, or when and where the setting is, or what has led up to this event, or what will happen next. In this way, we create our own version of a whole new story.

Visual images have always been a source of inspiration to authors and poets. In addition to Celia Rees above - who uses images to give her writing a strong sense of place - a great many of our contemporary children's authors use images such as photographs, illustrations, drawings, paintings and even films, animations and television programmes - to inspire their work. For example, part of the inspiration for Russell Hoban's teenage novel *The Trokeville Way* was a watercolour painting of a stone bridge over a river by Andrew Hislop - and a different version of the painting actually features in the book. Some of Ian Beck's illustrations for his own picture books have been informed by camera angles from the films of Alfred Hitchcock. At the end of this chapter, Michael Morpurgo talks about his novel *The Last Wolf* and explains how a specific image from Tate Britain informed the writing of the book.

The 'Gallery' section that appears in this chapter features a range of photocopiable images - photographs, illustrations, artwork - and a wide variety of subjects. For each of the images that feature there are detailed creative writing activity ideas. Yet these are only suggestions, and teachers are encouraged to use these images for their own purposes and activities, and also to allow children at times to write from these images in the way that they choose.

Any of the workshops that follow can be undertaken by children independently or by small groups and whole classes working with a teacher. For group and whole class sessions, a teacher or adult helper can act as scribe and collect any ideas, words or phrases on to the board or a sheet of paper as the children brainstorm their thoughts. This can be used as a source of ideas and words from which the children can later work.

The material that follows can be used directly with a class.

*　　　　*　　　　*

The following suggestions may be helpful as you are using an image to inspire writing:

- Write down every single idea and thought that comes to you, be it a word, phrase, sentence, piece of dialogue, or image (or even a whole series of images) or a feeling, memory, smell or taste, name of a character, description of a place or person - just jot down anything and everything you think of.
- Do not worry about spelling, punctuation or grammar - simply concentrate on getting the words down on the page.
- Try not to think about how these words and ideas are going to form a piece of writing, as you are just brainstorming at the moment; however, if you find yourself starting a story or a poem during the brainstorming stage, then that's fine - explore that idea.
- If it is an image (or series of images) that comes to mind - you can draw these if you want to.
- Once you have finished brainstorming, spend time reading over the notes that you have and go searching for material for a piece of writing - perhaps you have a phrase that could start a poem, or there might be a phrase that would make a good title, or an image that could serve as an opening of a story.
- Don't try to use everything you have written down - it isn't good to have too many ideas in a piece of writing - think of the phrase 'less is more'. Put the sheet of paper with the ideas you don't use in a file and come back to it another time when you need some ideas for writing.

WRITING FROM IMAGES - GENERAL WORKSHOP ACTIVITIES

Sourcing images

Magazines, Sunday newspapers, catalogues, brochures and postcards are all useful sources of images. Collect and keep those that you like - even create your own collage. You do not have to rush into writing about your image(s); perhaps mull over the image for a while and wait for the ideas to come to you. Experiment with the best form (or even genre) for the ideas - see 'Glossary - forms of writing'.

Visiting galleries

Classes can attend art galleries or museums, and do initial brainstorm workshop activities on location, which can later be developed in class. A number of galleries run educational programmes as well as writing workshops. See 'Questions' workshop below.

Questions

Teacher-led activity: teachers can choose from the following selection of general questions and ask children to apply some of these to an image - either from the 'Gallery' section or an image in the classroom, an art gallery or a museum. Teachers can write down some of the children's responses on a board or on a large sheet of paper. This brainstorming list can then serve as a basis for further discussion and/or for the children to refer to as they are developing their ideas into pieces of writing.

- What was your first thought, feeling or reaction to the image - and has it changed since you have spent time looking at it?
- Are there any features that you did not notice at first?
- Does it remind you of anything - or make you think of something else?
- How would you describe this picture?
- How would you describe the mood or atmosphere?
- How does it make you feel?
- If you could change the image in any way, what would you do?
- Who are the people in this picture? What are they doing? How do they feel at this moment? How do they feel about each other? What would they be saying if they were speaking? What thoughts are going through their minds? Where have they been/are they going? What will they do next? What question(s) would you like to ask these people?
- Where is this place? How does it feel to be there? Describe this place in terms of the senses - such as sight, smell, hearing and touch. What are the weather conditions? Is it hot, warm or cold? Is there a breeze blowing?
- When is this? What year? What time of year? What time of day?
- What is taking place - and, most importantly, why? What events led up to this, and what will happen next?

Teachers are encouraged to add further questions - as well as specific and relevant ones to the chosen image - to their list.

Before, during and after

Think of the image as a still from a film. Take time to look at it in detail and think about exactly what is going on. Is there a main event in the foreground and a less significant one in the background that is also worth considering? Write down some of your responses.

Then think of the BEFORE:

- What events led up to this picture?

Then think of the AFTER:

- What will happen next? How will events change or develop?

Write down a list of possibilities - or draw a series of further images - and then write a short story that tells of these events.

Change the picture

Add or remove certain things from your picture: characters, buildings, objects - anything. Change it around as you wish or merge details from a variety of other images. For example, you could place the characters in a different setting or introduce characters from another picture. Make it the picture that you want it to be for your piece of writing.

Characters

If there are people in a painting or photograph, you can build up a biography or character profile for one particular person (or even a group of people), using whatever clues there are in the picture as well as your imagination. Ask questions of that person - How old are they? Where do they/have they lived? What is her/his name? What is her/his background? What secrets might they have? What are their hopes, ambitions, problems, fears? Then write either a monologue in the voice of that character or a short story based around them. If there are a number of people in the image, imagine what their relationships are and how they feel about each other. Write a conversation between two of them. (Workshop adapted from the Tate Galleries' Visual Paths programme.)

Another character activity is to find a picture of a person that interests you. Imagine that character at different ages. You might want to consider - what lie did they tell at the age of 5? They were mentioned in a local newspaper when they were 15 - why? Write a letter that they sent at the age of 25 in which they apologise for something they did a long time before. Choose one of these to write about.

Forms and genres

Teacher-led activity: Colin Grigg of the Tate Galleries promotes the telling of stories from visual images in specific forms and genres. Imagine Leonardo Da Vinci's painting of the Mona Lisa - if you were to write about this character, you could do so in a variety of ways. It could be as a biographical sketch, a diary extract in the voice of Mona Lisa, a fictional short story or monologue, an exchange of letters, a poem, or even a short dramatic sketch between Da Vinci and his subject as he was painting her. Likewise, you could choose any of the images from the 'Gallery' section that follows and work out a story from the image and then tell the story in the style of a ghost or supernatural story, a newspaper report, a science fiction piece or whatever seems to work most naturally. Also see the 'Genres and Places' word wheel on p. 104 as well as 'Glossary - forms of writing'.

Mixing media

Teacher-led activity: another way of using different stimuli is to bring two together, such as a piece of music and an image. It is quite natural to appreciate images with music, as we regularly do this in the context of film or television. Teachers could choose one image from the following 'Gallery' section and one track from the accompanying CD. Teachers can then ask the pupils to examine the image closely as they are listening to the piece of music and to brainstorm all thoughts and ideas that come to them.

Alternatively, an artefact could be introduced with an image. For example, an old leather-bound diary could be used in conjunction with the photograph of the thatched cottage from the 'Gallery'. With the photograph, the children need to be encouraged to make connections between the two and to discover who owned the diary in this house, and what the diary owner's story might be - and can then go on to write some diary entries. (See 'Mix and Match Images' below.)

Pick an object

In a painting or picture choose an object - it can be anything at all, such as a tree or a cloud, a table or a rug. Write an autobiographical piece (or a free verse poem) in which you describe the object from its own point of view, but never mention what you are. If you were to be a tree, for a free verse poem you might begin: 'Once I lived under-ground/I burst through the soil/and I grew and I grew until . . .' (Workshop adapted from the Tate Galleries' Visual Paths programme.)

Put yourself in the picture

Imagine you are standing inside one particular photo/painting/illustration. Imagine what it is like to be there. Write a free verse poem in which you describe how you feel about being there, and the place - in terms of smells, sounds, sights, textures and so on - and consider: is the wind blowing, is it warm or cold and how would you describe the atmosphere? You might also wonder what is beyond the frame of the picture - are there details that the artist/illustrator/photographer didn't include?

Missing person

Choose a picture that features some people. Imagine that there is someone missing from this picture. Who is this person? Why are they not there? What happened? Write that person's story.

Mix and match images

Choose two compatible images from the 'Gallery' section that follows, for example, the picture of the boy on the bicycle p. 73 and the image of the city at night on p. 76, or even the girl with the baby on p. 65 and the picture of the thatched cottage on p. 68. What story emerges when you put such images together? Experiment with your own couplings. (See 'Mixing Media' above.)

THE GALLERY

Each image in this section can be photocopied. The blank space on each page with an image is intended for brainstorming ideas and notes.

For each image from the 'Gallery' there are a number of creative writing options to choose from, which can be adapted according to invidual needs. Or, children can be given the freedom to discover their own creative paths and consequently their own narratives, poems or other ideas for these images. The Glossary 'Forms of Writing' on p. 107 can help in providing specific forms if required.

IMAGE 1
A wedding

(photograph by Kenneth Bentley)

- Find a person from this picture that interests you. Create a biography for this person – their name, age, address, school, background, likes/dislikes, dreams, problems and ambitions. Write a monologue for this person in which s/he talks about something that has been on her/his mind for a long time.
- Imagine there is something unusual about this wedding. Perhaps everyone at the wedding knows about it, or just a few of them.
- Someone – who is not in this picture – carries this photograph around with them wherever they go. Why?
- Another wedding took place in this very spot on the same day 300 years before. Something unusual happened at that wedding. What was it? Write about it in a short story in the third person.

IMAGE 2
Girl with baby

(illustration by Peter Bailey)

- Why is this girl carrying a baby? Where has she run from? Where is she running to – and what will happen when she gets there? What is on her mind?
- This girl and her baby sister are escaping. From what or whom? What will happen to them? Imagine this scene is taking place:
  a) during a bomb raid in World War II;
  b) in Victorian Britain; or
  c) in five years from now.
- A TV drama opens with this image. Draw a storyboard for the next few scenes. Work out a plotline first.

IMAGE 3
Insects

(illustration by Ian Beck)

- As world-wide pollution increases over the next 100 years, a new breed of highly poisonous fly evolves. Write about this as either:
  a) a newspaper report; or
  b) a third-person science fiction story.
- Write a fantasy story in which humans have never existed and these insects (capable of speech and thought) dominate the world.
- Write about a day in the life of one of these insects – either as a diary entry, a monologue or rap poem.

IMAGE 4
Tottenham Court Road tube station

(photograph by Rob Vincent)

- Where are these people going? One of them is going to do something that would surprise you. Write about what happens as you follow that person.
- Science fiction narrative. Britain, the year 2200. Look closely at this picture. Can you see the image of a strange-looking man in the background? Imagine this image is on a giant monitor and that the man you can see controls an army-led political party that controls the country. Develop this scenario into a story, perhaps incorporating one or some of the people in the picture.
- Character biography – see first option in 'Image 1'.

IMAGE 5
Thatched cottage

- Use this cottage as the setting for a ghost or supernatural story with a difference. Exactly how it is different is up to you.
- Someone grew up here as a child. They are thinking back to a specific incident that took place here on a snowy January morning that they will never forget. Write a story in the first person in which that person tells of what happened on that day.
- This cottage is one of the main settings for a new film. What is the film about? First, write a short synopsis, and then either:
  a) do a storyboard for a scene that takes place here; or
  b) write the scene as a short piece of prose.

IMAGE 6
Elephant at circus

- Write a haiku poem about this event.
- Write a mini-saga – a 50-word story – about this event and why it is happening.
- What happens next? Begin a short story with the sentence 'As the crowd roared . . .'

IMAGE 7
'An Ancient Castle' by Sir Robert Ker Porter

- This castle is about to be attacked by an invading army. Describe the event in a short story in the third person.
- Write a free verse poem in which you capture the mood and atmosphere of this painting. Try to use descriptive language – with some metaphors or similes.
- Write a conversation that these two guards may be having.
- Using this castle as a setting, write a fantasy story about a land that is inhabited by mythic creatures.

IMAGE 8
Taking a boat out to sea

(photograph by Rob Vincent)

- Write a short poem or a piece of descriptive prose in which you convey how it feels to be at this place at this time. Use some of the senses – hearing, smell and sight. Make a list of descriptive words or phrases for each sense and then merge them all together in your piece.
- Write a mini-saga (a story in exactly 50 words) in which you tell the story of these three people and their boat. You will have to work out the storyline first – detailing where they are going and why, and what will happen when they get there. In your first draft you will probably write more than 50 words. Trim it down in the second or third draft.
- Imagine that the event in this photograph is the middle of a short adventure story. You have to work out where these people have been before this, and where they will go in their boat. Work out a full plan. Give them names, discover how they know each other. As this will be an adventure story, inject some excitement into your story – perhaps they have discovered a secret, or someone is following them, or they are following someone else, or someone has been kidnapped. You decide.
- This is an image of the opening to a story, about a day at the sea that goes wrong. Write that story. With this, don't even brainstorm, go straight into the writing and see where the story goes.
- Imagine these three are going to an island off the coast, an island they visit often. Why do they go there? What is there? Write their story.

- Imagine that this photograph is a still from a film. Set the image into motion in your mind, and think:

  Where are these boys going?

  What are they talking about?

  Why are they taking the boat out?

  Quickly give the three boys names – or call them 'A', 'B' and 'C' until you can think of their names. Then get them talking to each other. Write the conversation that they will have when they are rowing out.

IMAGE 9
Cat's funeral

(illustration by Peter Bailey)

- Write a rhyming poem about this event.
- Who is the man watching this event? Write about the funeral from his point of view.
- Write a short story in the third person in which you tell what happens next.
- Imagine this is a still from a short animated film. Write a storyboard for the film. First, work out a storyline – and include the events that take place before and after this image.

IMAGE 10
Boy on bicycle

(photograph by Rob Vincent)

- Immediately after the photograph was taken, this boy witnessed an event taking place. What was it, and how is it going to affect the boy's life? Write this as a short story in either the third or first person.
- Look into the future of this boy's life. What significant event will happen to him at the age of 18? Write about this as a newspaper article.
- *Group activity.* This boy is one of a number of characters for a new TV drama for young people. Who are the other characters? Develop your ideas about this boy first, and then write about the other characters. Where will the story be set – at a school, a youth club, or in a certain street? Improvise scenes in which members of your group take on the characters of the TV drama. Record these and transcribe your ideas. Develop your script from there.

IMAGE 11
'Heads of Six of Hogarth's Servants' by William Hogarth

- Imagine these are all ghosts of people that used to work in an old hotel in a city. Write a comedy piece (short play or story) in which the modern-day owner of the hotel advertises his hotel as a 'haunted dwelling' only to discover one night that it is!

- Again, imagine these people are all ghosts. Once a year they all come back to haunt the ancestor of someone who was once very cruel to them. Write this as a short story or drama.
- These people all witnessed a famous event in history. Which one was it? Tell the story of that event in the voice of one of these characters.

IMAGE 12
Children celebrating VE Day, 1945

(photograph from Imperial War Museum)

- Who are these two girls? Where are they? Why are they waving flags? What is going to happen to them? Write their story in the third person.
- Why are these children waving flags? What is the event? Write a monologue in the voice of one of these two girls as a teenager thinking back to that day.
- These two girls are separated the day after this photograph is taken. Why? What happened? They don't meet up for another ten years. Write a short play in which they meet and discuss everything that has happened to them.

IMAGE 13
Aerial view of central London at night

(photograph by Rob Vincent)

- Write a free verse poem that captures the mood of a city at night. Use some expressive metaphors, similes and verbs.
- Imagine this is London in the year 2560. Write about an event that takes place one night in this city.
- Someone is being chased through the streets. Why is s/he being chased? Who is chasing her/him? What will happen?

IMAGE 14
Mr Nice and Mr Nasty

(illustration by Ian Beck)

- Choose one of these two characters. Rather than 'Mr Nice' or 'Mr Nasty', give him a real name, but keep his personality and put him in a difficult situation. Write this as a short drama or short story.
- Mr Nice and Mr Nasty (or even Ms Nice and Ms Nasty) are two aspects of the same person – someone who can be very cruel but also extremely kind. Write a poem or short story about this character.
- What would happen if these two characters met? Write a short drama for these two characters. Improvise a scene or two with a partner.

IMAGE 15
Child sitting at table in cottage

(photograph by Rob Vincent)

- A meeting is about to take place here to discuss something of great importance. Write this as a short drama.
- The mother of this child is upstairs frantically packing as, unexpectedly, they have to leave the house and go on a long journey. In a short story in the third person, explain why they have to leave and where they will go.
- A teenager has a recurring dream of being a child again and sitting at a table with empty chairs. S/he has never been to this house. What else happens in the dream? Why is the dream taking place? Is it a false memory or a premonition? Write a piece about this either as a short story or as a free verse poem.
- While the child waits in the kitchen, one of his parents goes to collect the post, in which there is a letter that is going to change their lives. Tell that story.

IMAGE 16
Three pairs of shoes

- Choose one pair of shoes. Write a story that begins 'These shoes have travelled over 1,000 miles and this is their story . . .' *or* write a humorous free verse poem from the shoes' point of view, telling the story of their owner.
- These shoes belong to a small family – a husband, a wife and their young daughter. They have been travelling a long distance by train. Where are they going – or where do they hope to go? Why are they making this journey?
- Who owns these shoes? Write a three stanza free verse poem. In each stanza write about the owner of the shoes. You might want to begin each stanza with something along the lines of 'The owner of those shoes is . . .'
- This photograph appeared in a newspaper. All that was found of these people were their shoes on a beach. What happened to them? Write a newspaper article that tells their story.

IMAGE 17
Map of Southridge village

(by Bethan Matthews)

- Something happens that will affect the entire community of this village. Tell this story from the point of view of one of the villagers.
- This is the setting for a TV drama or soap opera for young people. Develop four characters (two girls, two boys) and write a few scenes.
- The locals in this area are unaware of an event that took place on this site some 800 years ago. By accident, one of the locals discovers some information in a nearby library that begins their journey to solve the mystery.

Girl and boy in a kitchen

(illustration by Peter Bailey)

- Who are these people? Where are they? What are they doing? Gather some details in note form for a while and then write a short story in the third person that features this scenario.
- Begin a short story with this scenario in the first person, from either the boy's or the girl's point of view. Just begin writing without any planning – but do stop and make notes as you go along if you need to.
- This event takes place in the middle of a story. Before you begin writing the story in either the first or third person, work out what events might take place before and after.

IMAGE 19
Junk yard

(photograph by Rob Vincent)

- Make a long list of the kinds of things that get taken to junk yards – cars, chairs, televisions, mattresses, sofas and so on. Put some of these together to form a 'scrap rap' or a rhyming poem. John Foster has written his own 'Recycling Rap' (*Standing on the Sidelines*, Oxford University Press) – why not write your own?
- Open a short story in this junk yard at night – it could be a horror story, a fantasy, a ghost story, whatever you choose.
- Write a short monologue from the point of view of a car in this junk yard.
- Write a mini-saga (a story told in exactly 50 words) about the life of a car that ends its life in this junk yard.

IMAGE 20
'Punch on May Day' by Benjamin Robert Haydon

- Write a short piece in which you describe life in this London street in the nineteenth century.
- Choose one of the characters from this painting and imagine you are following that person immediately after this event. You discover that they are up to no good. Where will they go? What will they do? Write a short story in which you recount that person's actions and how you feel about it.
- One of the people in this painting is your ancestor. Tell a short story in the third person that sums up their life.

IMAGE 21
Holland House Library, 23 October 1940

- Where is this? Why has it happened? What is the story behind this image? Write the story as a newspaper report.
- Write a mini-saga (a story told in exactly 50 words) that tells of this event.
- This library was bombed the night before. The library was just closing as the bombs dropped. Write a short story in the first person from the point of view of one of the librarians as they were locking up for the night.

IMAGE 22
'Wolf' by Henri Gaudier-Brzeska

- Write a fairy tale in which a wolf is the hero. Use some of the traditional fairy ingredients, such as a moral, the number three or seven, wishes, a happy ending, good/bad characters.
- Write a short story set 400 years ago, which begins with a wolf entering the back door of a farmhouse one dark evening.
- A wolf escapes from a small rural zoo in the present day. What will happen? Write this either as a newspaper report or as a short story in the first person, from the point of view of the wolf.

IMAGE 1

IMAGE 2

IMAGE 3

IMAGE 4

IMAGE 5

IMAGE 6

IMAGE 7

IMAGE 8

IMAGE 9

IMAGE 10

IMAGE 11

IMAGE 12

IMAGE 13

IMAGE 14

IMAGE 15

IMAGE 16

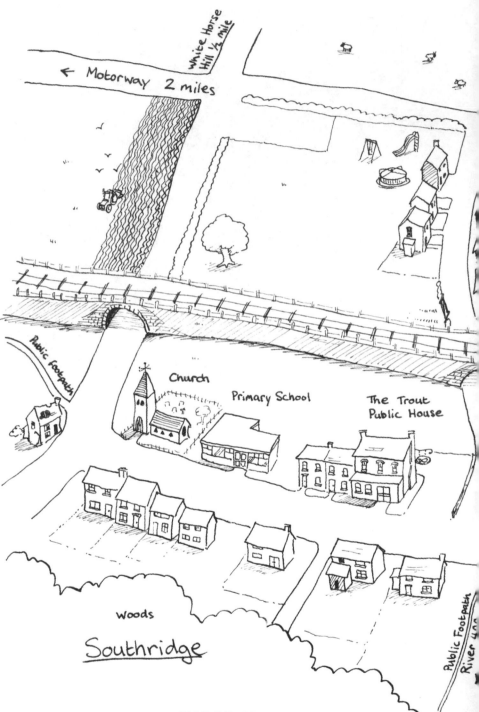

IMAGE 17

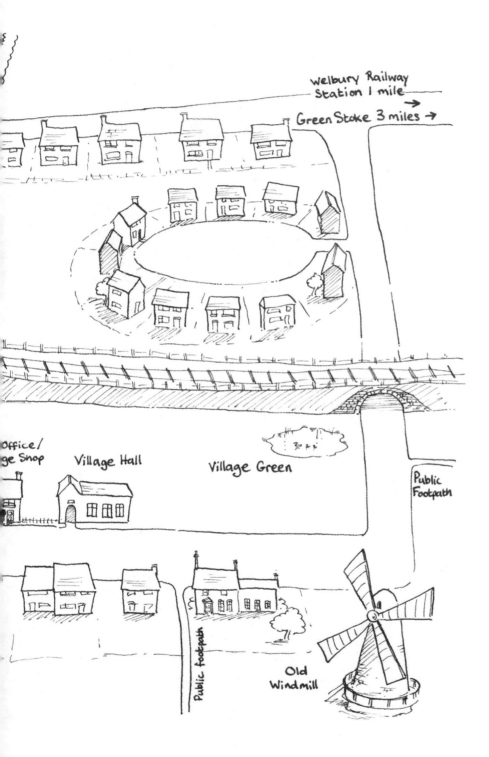

Welbury Railway
Station 1 mile →

Green Stoke 3 miles →

Office/
ge Shop

Village Hall

Village Green

Public
Footpath

Public Footpath

Old
Windmill

IMAGE 18

IMAGE 19

IMAGE 20

IMAGE 21

IMAGE 22

*   *   *

Author Michael Morpurgo regularly uses pictures and paintings as a source of inspiration for his stories. Here he discusses how a drawing of a wolf by a Polish artist helped to inspire his novel *The Last Wolf*:

> There are always a number of different strands that I weave together to form a book, a weaving of truths to make a cloth of fiction. One strand of *The Last Wolf* came about as a result of my time as writer-in-residence at Tate Britain. It was a drawing of a wolf by Henri Gaudier-Brzeska. The drawing is of a scrawny-looking wolf, and looks more like a greyhound than a wolf. And because of this I realised how the character in the book could disguise the wolf – by shaving off its coat – which would enable him to smuggle it onto a boat travelling from Scotland to America, as I wanted the wolf to re-discover its natural home. So this picture made the denouement of the whole story possible.

The following extract from *The Last Wolf* explains how the wolf – known as Charlie – was sheared:

> Tame though he now was, and biddable too, and in many respects much like any other large dog, there could be no doubt that Charlie did indeed now resemble what in fact he unmistakably was, a wolf. I knew well enough that almost no creature is more instantly recognisable than a wolf, and that none inspires more fear, nor more hatred either. Discovery would mean certain death for both of us, wolf and rebel alike, a circumstance I tried to explain to Charlie as I set about the business of disguising him.
>
> I think I should never have discovered how this might be accomplished at all, had not my eye fallen one evening on a pair of discarded sheep shears hanging on the wall of the croft. I burned the rust off in the fire, sharpened the sheep shears on a stone, and set to work on Charlie. But Charlie made it plain that this was an indignity he deeply resented. He would growl at me and back away, refusing to stand still for me. I knew full well that I could not restrain him against his will, for he was by now far too strong for me. So I resorted to bribery, as I often did with Charlie. I discovered that if I coaxed him almost constantly with rabbit meat he would, albeit unwillingly, stand and endure the sheep shears.
>
> Until I began to cut his hair, I never imagined a wolf could grow so much of it and so thick. When, after some hours, I had done with my clipping, Charlie had taken on the appearance more of a bedraggled deerhound than a wolf. Although on close examination, his great webbed feet and his amber eyes might betray him, I was satisfied that he no longer had the shape and form of a wolf, that he might indeed pass for a large hound. I can mind how he stood there in his humiliation looking up at me out of baleful, accusing eyes, his tail between his legs. I would not, I thought, be easily forgiven. In this I was mistaken. It seemed not to be in Charlie's nature to bear a grudge, and very soon we were once again the best of friends.

MICHAEL MORPURGO
Illustrated by Michael Foreman
The Last Wolf

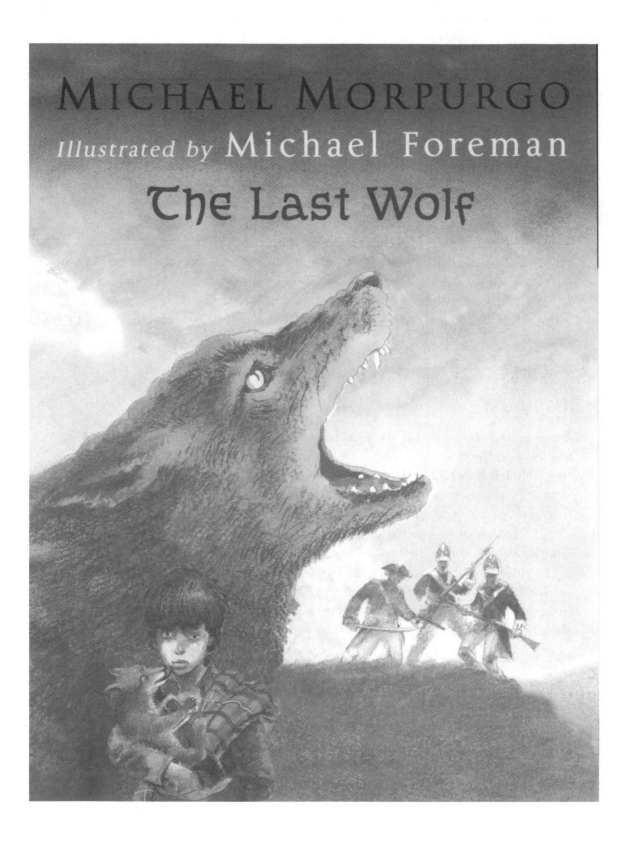

Music

'Music is a very powerful inspiration.'
(Berlie Doherty, novelist)

'Playing music can establish a creative writing mood.
t transports the class gently into another mode of thinking where thoughts drift,
surprises appear and the imagination starts to wander and to wonder.'
(Pie Corbett, poet/educational consultant)

WRITING WITH MUSIC

Music can be composed with many purposes in mind – such as to evoke an atmosphere, mood or emotion or to conjure up a place, a person or an event. Composers have written music that impersonates the sounds of trains and animals, as well as music that captures the atmospheres of market places, oceans, cities and even outer space. But music can do even more than this: it can tell stories. Consider these two celebrated twentieth-century compositions which have narrative qualities – George Gershwin's *Rhapsody in Blue* (which the composer himself described as 'a sort of musical kaleidoscope of America') and Prokofiev's *Peter and the Wolf* – in which specific instruments of the orchestra represent various characters from the Russian fairy tale.

In both film and television, music is one of a number of key elements employed to tell a story – and it is not simply an accompaniment, but an integral aspect of the narrative. It is hard to imagine such films as Spielburg's *Jaws* or Hitchcock's *Psycho* without their distinctive and haunting soundtracks.

Like the image, music has always been a source of inspiration for writers. Some authors, like Russell Hoban and Norman Silver, have been known to listen to specific pieces of music before they have begun their writing for the day, as they have found that it helps to put them in a creative frame of mind. Other authors, although it is rare, actually have music playing as they are writing. One author who has actually written fiction to music is Berlie Doherty; at the end of this chapter she explains in detail how music features in her work. This is followed by three pieces of writing – inspired by the first track on the CD – from three young writers at St Andrew's School in Wantage, Oxfordshire.

Instrumental music is a popular and most productive stimulus in creative writing workshops with both adults and young writers. What music has to offer writing is that it is such a potent source of material. All of the ideas, moods, emotions, images and memories that instrumental music so readily suggests can be transposed into words and phrases, and ultimately narratives, poems and other forms of writing. It is therefore the aim of this chapter to encourage children to *see* and *react to* music and to learn how to *translate* music – abstract sounds, melodies, patterns and rhythms – into their own words and ideas.

On a more practical note, children do find it very useful if the piece of music for the workshop can be played twice (see 'Talking music' below). Ideas tend to flow more freely on a second hearing. And clearly, as with all writing, full concentration is vital, and it may help some children to close their eyes initially. It will be necessary for there to be a few moments' silence after the piece has been played, so that the class can continue to form, shape and record their thoughts and ideas. The result will essentially be raw material, a mass of thoughts and notes or a 'stream of consciousness' that will then have to be shaped and developed into a coherent piece of writing. At this stage, the pupils could either be allowed to decide for themselves how to develop their ideas, or teachers can suggest a range of forms. (See Glossary: Forms of Writing, p. 107). The following stages – which can be read directly to a class – might be of use when writing with music:

- Write down every single idea and thought that comes to you, be it a word, phrase, sentence, piece of dialogue, image (or even a whole series of images), a feeling, memory, smell or taste, name of a character, description of a place or person – just jot down anything and everything you think of.
- Do not worry about spelling or punctuation or grammar – simply concentrate on getting the words down on the page.
- Do not worry about how these words and ideas are going to form a piece of writing, as you are only brainstorming at the moment; however, if you find yourself starting a story or a poem during this stage, then that's fine, explore that idea.
- If it is an image (or series of images) that comes to mind, you can draw these if you want to.
- Once you have finished brainstorming, spend time reading over the notes that you have and go searching for raw materials for a piece of writing – perhaps you have a phrase that could start a poem, or there might be a phrase that would make a good title, or an image that could serve as an opening of a story.
- Don't try to use everything you have written down – it isn't good to have too many ideas in a piece of writing – think of the phrase 'less is more'. Put the sheet of paper with the ideas you don't use in a file and come back to it another time when you need some ideas for writing.
- Sometimes it is helpful to hear a piece of music a number of times – ask your teacher if you can borrow a recording of the piece so that you can listen to it at home or with headphones in the classroom.

And finally, when choosing music to play in a writing workshop, teachers will need to consider the following:

- Choose a piece no more than 3–4 minutes in length; alternatively, you could play a longer piece and fade the volume down after 3–4 minutes.
- Instrumental music is more appropriate as lyrics will either direct the imagination too much or not stimulate the imagination at all.
- Pick music that is relevant to children – there are so many genres to choose from, from world music to classical, ambient to film soundtracks.
- Film soundtracks are often a great source of music for workshops – and are often very atmospheric, evoking a range of emotions.
- Listen to a piece a few times before the workshop and jot down what ideas come to you and be ready to use these with the class.

WRITING WITH MUSIC -
GENERAL WORKSHOP ACTIVITIES

Talking music

After the music has been played once and the class have brainstormed their ideas onto paper, a discussion can follow in which these types of issues are discussed:

- Did you like/dislike the piece? Why?
- How did it make you feel? Did it bring out certain emotions?
- How would you describe the mood or atmosphere of the piece?
- When and where does it make you think of?
- How would you describe the music? What style is it?
- Does it remind you of anything?
- Did it bring back any memories for you?
- Did it inspire any mental images/a story?
- Did any words/phrases spring to mind?

From here, teachers may choose to play the piece a second time for the class to generate further ideas.

Questions

Teacher-led activity: as children are listening to a piece of music they can pose a set of standard general questions to help them discover ideas. Simply by considering such questions as Who? What? Where? When? Why? ideas should start to formulate regarding either characters, events, places or times as well as images or emotions, atmospheres, words or phrases. Children can write these questions – Who? What? etc. . . . – at the top of their sheets as prompts for when they are listening and responding to the piece of music. From here, teachers may choose to discuss each question in turn with the group and collect ideas on the board.

Creating characters

As you are listening to your piece of music, imagine the music is a fictional character. Try as hard as you can to visualise the character in your mind's eye. First think about these questions and then write down your responses: What does s/he look like? What is s/he doing as you see her/him? How old is s/he? Where does s/he come from? What makes her/him happy/unhappy? Write as detailed a character profile as you can for the character.

   If a story or situation for that character does not come to mind automatically, write either a diary entry for that person in which s/he describes some of her/his innermost feelings, or write about what s/he wants more than anything else, and how s/he will go about trying to get it.

Fantasia

In the animated Disney film *Fantasia*, music is expressed graphically – as colours, patterns and shapes. Close your eyes as you listen to a piece of music and imagine the sounds in such colours, patterns and shapes. Try to describe the sensation in words – write down all your thoughts – words, phrases, anything you think of. Even draw or doodle any images, patterns or shapes you imagine. Be really adventurous with your ideas. Afterwards, choose the words and phrases you like best and work these into a free verse poem.

'What if . . .'

As you are listening to a piece of music, imagine what if the piece of music was:

- an event;
- an animal;
- a place;
- a memory;
- a dream;
- an animated/live action film;
- a story book for younger readers.

Develop one of these ideas.

Soundtracks

What can you see as the music plays? Imagine it is the soundtrack or the background music to a film or television drama. Watch the images as they form in your mind's eye. Can you see a person or group of people or a setting or an event taking place? If it helps, close your eyes – which may help you to visualise the image more clearly. Don't worry about writing anything immediately, just follow the image for as long as you can and then later gather your thoughts onto paper.

Feeling music

With a piece of music that is strong in atmosphere or emotion, you can concentrate as the track is playing on how it makes you feel. Does it excite you? Does it scare you? Does it make you feel peaceful and mellow, or angry and annoyed, or thoughtful and reflective? Once you have explored your emotions, write down any words or even images that come to mind.

Mixing media

See 'Mixing Media' in the 'Images' chapter on p. 55.

Music as a touchstone

As the music is playing, think back over your life and consider various memories and events from your past. Find a particular event/moment/image and brainstorm all ideas, words, feelings that you can. Later on, structure your ideas into an autobiographical piece of writing.

BACKGROUND INFORMATION TO THE CD

The music on the accompanying CD can be used in a variety of ways:

- by following some of the general workshop activities above;
- by doing some of the specific writing activities related to each track on the CD that follow;
- by teachers/workshop leaders introducing their own writing activities to tracks from the CD;
- by pupils freewriting/brainstorming/improvising as they are listening to a piece of music, and then shaping their ideas into forms of their own choice (see bullet point stages in the 'Writing with Music' section earlier in this chapter).

The compact disc features three soundscapes and five pieces of music. Each track has been specially composed for this book and is to be actively used in creative writing workshops. Quite deliberately, the styles and featured instruments vary from track to track. These pieces will help to nurture mental imagery, atmospheres and moods – and one single piece will most likely stimulate a wide variety of responses from a class, as each person hears, interprets and responds to music in their own subjective way.

The first three pieces are soundscapes, which contain both music and sound effects:

Track 1
SOUNDSCAPE: 'City Trains' (James Carter/Mark Hawkins)
Over a minimalist piano motif, there are the sounds of trains arriving at a station, passengers disembarking and walking through subways. In the middle of the piece, city sounds are heard – such as roadworks, traffic and pedestrians. The piece concludes with the sounds of trains leaving a railway station.

Track 2
SOUNDSCAPE: 'Big Bright Moon' (James Carter)
With a minimal ambient vibraphone motif, the sound effects – such as birds, rain, church bells and footsteps – suggest night-time in the countryside.

Track 3
SOUNDSCAPE: 'Time Piece' (Kenny Stone)
Featuring sporadic ambient, ethereal sounds and a soothing heartbeat, there is a sequence of different sounds featured throughout, from footsteps to a waterfall to children playing in a school playground.

The five instrumentals cover a variety of musical genres:

Track 4
MUSIC: 'Fisher Boy' (Mark Hawkins)
A meandering, gentle and reflective piano piece.

Track 5
MUSIC: 'Jangle' (James Carter)
A celebratory, upbeat African-style piece with percussion, guitars, marimbas and drums.

Track 6
MUSIC: 'Not So Wicked' (Mark Hawkins)
A slow, haunting, dream-like piece with a gentle rhythm.

Track 7
MUSIC: 'War Bird' (Mark Hawkins)
An aggressive, hypnotic and frenetic piece.

Track 8
MUSIC: 'The Lemming Years' (James Carter)
A slow, lilting and atmospheric piece performed on electric guitars and keyboards.

All tracks recorded and produced by Mark Hawkins and James Carter, except 'Time Piece' – recorded and produced by Kenny Stone and Mark Hawkins. The compact disc is a Stereo Architects of Sound production.

RELATED WORKSHOP ACTIVITIES FOR TRACKS ON THE CD

It is a good idea if teachers and workshop leaders do not mention the title of a piece before it is played, as it might give too much unwanted direction to the children's writing early on. Also, it is strongly recommended that the chosen piece is played twice, as generally children discover more ideas during the second playing.

Track 1
SOUNDSCAPE: 'City Trains'

- Imagine this is the soundtrack for a film, a thriller that you are writing. Your main character is arriving by train in a city. Is s/he pursuing someone, or being pursued? What is taking place? Try to visualise the film in your mind's eye. Once you know the plot, write a few short scenes for your film, or alternatively, tell this as a short story.
- As you listen, try to find a rhythm that you can use for a rhyming poem. In your poem you may choose to write about the journey of a train, or the journey of someone travelling into a city, or simply the events that take place during a day in the city.

- A city is the setting for a short crime story. Someone is arriving in the city by train. They walk through the subway and up into the city. Eventually, they leave again by train. What crime did they commit in the city? What took place? Will they ever be caught? Listen to this piece and discover the story as you listen.

Track 2
SOUNDSCAPE: 'Big Bright Moon'

- Picture a small, remote village. It is a cold night with a full moon. Something takes place. What is it? Write about it in a short story which you begin with some descriptive and atmospheric writing. Let your reader know how it feels to be there. Or write about the events of the night in a newspaper report.
- Someone is looking out of a window at the night outside. Write what s/he sees in a free verse poem/piece of prose or even a diary entry. Use inventive, expressive and descriptive language – with metaphors and similes.
- Someone thinks back to one night over and over again, as something significant happened. In a first person short story, let your narrator explain the events.
- It is night. Someone is walking through the snow. Where is s/he going? Write an atmospheric piece in which you describe this person's journey.

Track 3
SOUNDSCAPE: 'Time Piece'

- You are sitting on a park bench in a city with your eyes closed concentrating on all the sounds that are going on around you. Write down every sound you hear. Now write a free verse poem that evokes the atmosphere of this city, but mainly in terms of sounds – try not to include much physical description.
- Someone is walking through a park in a town. As you listen to the sounds, imagine what is going through their mind – what thoughts, events, emotions and conversations. Once you have brainstormed your ideas, write about that person's experiences in a monologue.
- Imagine this is a soundtrack to a short film on television. Write or draw anything that comes into your mind's eye as you are listening. From here, either create a pictorial storyboard or a short story.

Track 4
MUSIC: 'Fisher Boy'

- Imagine someone is looking at a photograph of a group of people. Who is this person? Why are they holding the photograph? Who is in the photograph? Where is this person now? Write about the memory that the photograph evokes in a piece of prose.
- Imagine someone is sitting at a table by a window. They open a diary in front of them and write a whole page for that day. What do they write?
- Imagine this piece is the soundtrack to a memory of your own. Watch that memory in your mind's eye and then brainstorm all your thoughts. Choose the right form for your ideas. (See Glossary: Forms of Writing, p. 107.)

Track 5
MUSIC: 'Jangle'

- Someone is running through a market, upsetting all the stalls of fruit and vegetables. Why? What is happening?
- A carnival is taking place. What is being celebrated? Describe the scene – the colours, the people, the dancing, the movements, the sounds in a free verse poem or as a piece of prose.
- Imagine this piece of music is playing over the opening sequence to a film. What will the film be about? Try to visualise scenes and images from the film. Make a storyboard for the film.

Track 6
MUSIC: 'Not So Wicked'

- Imagine this is the soundtrack to someone's dream. What images/events would there be? Write this as a short piece of prose or as a free verse poem.
- You are walking in a building somewhere. Is it a long corridor or a large room or a basement? Is it a church or a temple or a disused warehouse or a disused indoor swimming pool or even a cave? Is it real or a dream? Write down descriptions of the place and how you feel about being there. Develop the piece however you wish.
- Imagine a film is playing in your mind's eye. There is a character walking slowly through a city. S/he looks scared and threatened as people and cars rush past her/him. What is going through this person's mind at this precise moment? Develop this scenario as either a short story or as a short film.

Track 7
MUSIC: 'War Bird'

- You are running down a street at night. Why are you running? Where are you running to or from? What can you see as you hear this music? Write a free verse poem or piece of prose in the first person. You could write in the present continuous tense and begin with something along the lines of 'It's night, it's dark and I'm running . . .'
- Imagine a film is playing in your mind's eye. You can see a back street in a city. It is night. There are two people – one is chasing the other. Follow them and discover what is happening. Write this as a short screenplay or story.
- In a futuristic city, the night sky is filled with unusual machines. There are monorail trains zooming across the horizon. Nobody is walking on the streets below, there are only car-like vehicles. There is a sudden explosion. What is happening? Write this as a short story.

Track 8
MUSIC: 'The Lemming Years'

- Two people are travelling by rowing boat on the sea on a cold and starry winter's night. They arrive at a small fishing village very early in the morning, when it is still dark. Who are they? What are they up to? Write their story in a third person short story, and begin as they are starting to row ashore.

- Imagine this is the opening piece of music for a new radio play. The opening scene takes place in a boat off the coast of Scotland. There are two people in the boat. Think: Who are these two people? What are they doing? Where they going? What problem are they about have? How will they solve it? Remember to include sound effects in your piece – for example, sounds of the water lapping, seagulls and the wind. (To see how action and dialogue are laid out, see the script of *Kensuke's Kingdom* on p. 26.)

- You are in a boat on the sea in the dark on a cold and cloudless starry night. The water is calm, and gently bobbing your boat. Write about this experience in a free verse poem or as a piece of prose in the present tense, in which you describe the cold, the sky, the darkness, the stars, the water, the overall atmosphere and the sensation of being there at that time.

- Imagine you are watching a documentary about the far north – and you can see images of ice sheets, of mountains covered in ice and snow, of the sky – showing permanent day, and maybe even the enchanting northern lights. Dwell upon these images. Turn some of these ideas into a free verse poem or a piece of prose.

*   *   *

Here, novelist Berlie Doherty explains how music features in her writing:

> A few years ago a group of musicians called The Lindsay String Quartet wanted to do a concert for children, and they asked me if I would write a story around the sort of music that they play. I listened to a piece of music by the French composer Debussy, his String Quartet in G minor, and immediately pictures started coming into my mind – I could see somebody running, searching for something. I could see streets of houses, and then dark moors. I could see a night sky. I could hear a refrain that made me think of the words *midnight man*, and I could hear another refrain like a dog barking softly. As I was listening to the music I was writing all this down, and then I drew a line under the words *Midnight Man* and started straight away to write the story-poem.
>
> The Lindsays performed the piece at their Christmas concert, with an actress reading my words. Because the pictures in my head were so strong, I wondered if *The Midnight Man* might make the text for a picture book. I sent it to Walker Books and they said yes straight away. Very soon they sent me Ian Andrew's ideas for the artwork and I knew that he and their designer were going to make a beautifully atmospheric book of it.
>
> The following year the Lindsay String Quartet invited me to write another story for their Christmas concert. This time I listened to a haunting piece of music by the Czech composer Smetana, the String Quartet No. 1 in E minor, *From My Life*. I remember listening to it in my car, sitting overlooking the

Derbyshire hills, and it seemed to be so much part of that landscape that I knew I wanted to write a story that was set there. The music moved between the emotions of joy and sadness, loss and finding; sometimes it seemed to be about dancing, and sometimes it seemed to be about loneliness. I could hear a refrain of three sad notes in it, as if a voice was asking *Where am I? Who am I? Where are you?* I could see ice and darkness and sunlight, and I thought about the caverns nearby where a rare and beautiful stone called Blue John is mined. I decided to invent a character called *Blue John*, a boy created out of stone, and to make up a kind of fairy story about him.

This time I worked very closely with the music, listening to it many times and following its moods exactly. I followed the notes in the score and wrote the story to fit in with the stops and starts, the quiet and loud parts, and sometimes allowed the notes and the words to fit together exactly, so the actor and actress would read it like a spoken song.

So *Blue John* had two lives – a piece of music, and a story. I wanted to know if, like *Midnight Man*, it could have three, so I sent the story to Puffin Books, and they commissioned Tim Clarey to illustrate it as an exquisite picture book for older children. I sent him a recording of the music to see if it would inspire him in the same way that it had inspired me.

Music and stories can work the other way round, too. One of my daughters is a professional musician, and she set *The Midnight Man* to her own music to be performed live at concerts. In her version my speaking voice, her singing voice and the voices of the harp, the violin, cello, flute and clarinet weave in and out in a sort of sound picture. I had been inspired by Debussy, and she in turn was inspired by my words.

She also set a shortened version of my novel *Daughter of the Sea* to music for the same kind of instruments. As well as my readings, she sings sections of the text without making any changes to the words at all. You can hear part of it on her website, www.sallydoherty.com, and maybe you could work together with musicians to produce the same kind of music/story.

Now the Lindsays have just given me another commission, for Christmas 2001. This time they have chosen the music themselves. It's a piece by another Czech composer, Janacek, called The Kreutzer Sonata. The music is actually based on a story by the Russian writer Tolstoy! Of course, I daren't read it in case it stops my own imagination flowing! I haven't yet started to write my story. This is quite scarey, of course, but I know one thing for sure. The music will inspire me. It always does.

Music is a very powerful inspiration. If you want to try writing to music yourself, I advise you to find a piece that you don't know, otherwise you'll hum along to it. It mustn't have words, or they will distract you. As you listen, jot down the pictures and the moods that come into your head. Just let the words flow – don't try to shape them into sentences or into a story yet. Then look through your list and see what you've got. Listen to the music again, building up the ideas. Then just write, without the music. Let the words sing.

Berlie Doherty
September 2001

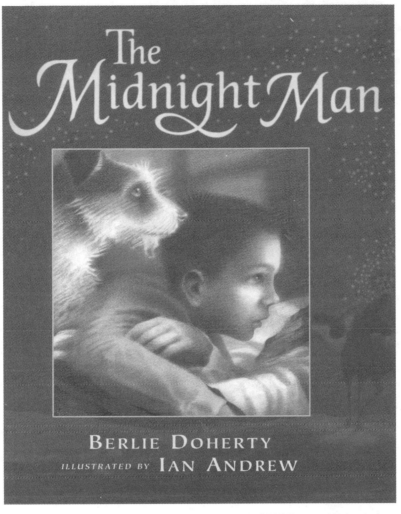

The Midnight Man, Walker Books (1998) Illustrated by Ian Andrew

The introduction to *The Midnight Man* by Berlie Doherty (Walker Books):

> Every night, when Harry and Mister Dog
> are asleep, someone comes riding by.
> Mister Dog opens one eye and grunts.
> Harry opens one eye and yawns.
> They both sit up
> and gaze out of the window,
> and this is what they see . . .
>
> The midnight man comes
> riding through the town
> on his midnight horse
> with its hushing hooves.
> His cloak of whispers
> swirls around like sighs.
> On his hip is a sack of stars.

A Figure

Standing in a clearing
In a sunlit wood
Water rushing down a creek
A field mouses feeble squeak
I see a lovely figure standing up ahead
She's wearing robes of green
I think she is a nature queen
I try to reach her but to see her smile.
and gently, slowly fade away
I run after her like a crazy dog
only to see a bare rock a clearing
And a lonely stray dog.
I feel all is lost like a lonely man.
The beautiful woman
gone from all eyes to see.

by Rosie
year 6

Magic

In the car out of the window
What you see is magic,
A waterfall so high you can not
see the top.
A market so crowded you can not
see anything.
But alas you see a snake
slithering across the sand
on the beach.
So beautiful, so lovely
Like a piece of art.
No rain no storm,
So silent,
You think yourself in a
different world.

by Annika

year 6

Traffic.

Racing by Zoom, Zoom!!

Accidents everywhere when people drive too fast. The

Fuel station where Grown ups. fill up the monsters with drink.

Finsh for the night, everything is quiet.

In the mornins. people get ready and get in

Car Zoom Zoom Beep Beep Crush Crush!

by Olivia

Word Wheel 1:
Genres and Places

These word wheels are to be cut out and assembled with brass clips.

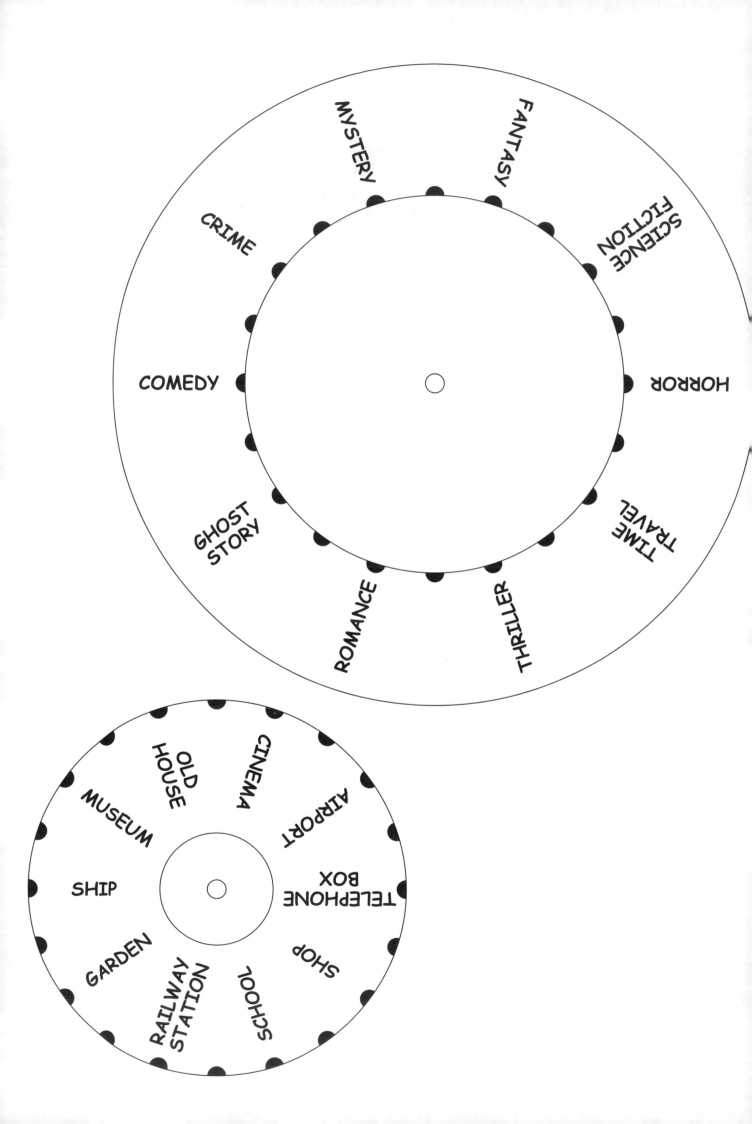

Word Wheel 2:
Scenarios and
Forms of Writing

These word wheels are to be cut out and assembled with brass clips.

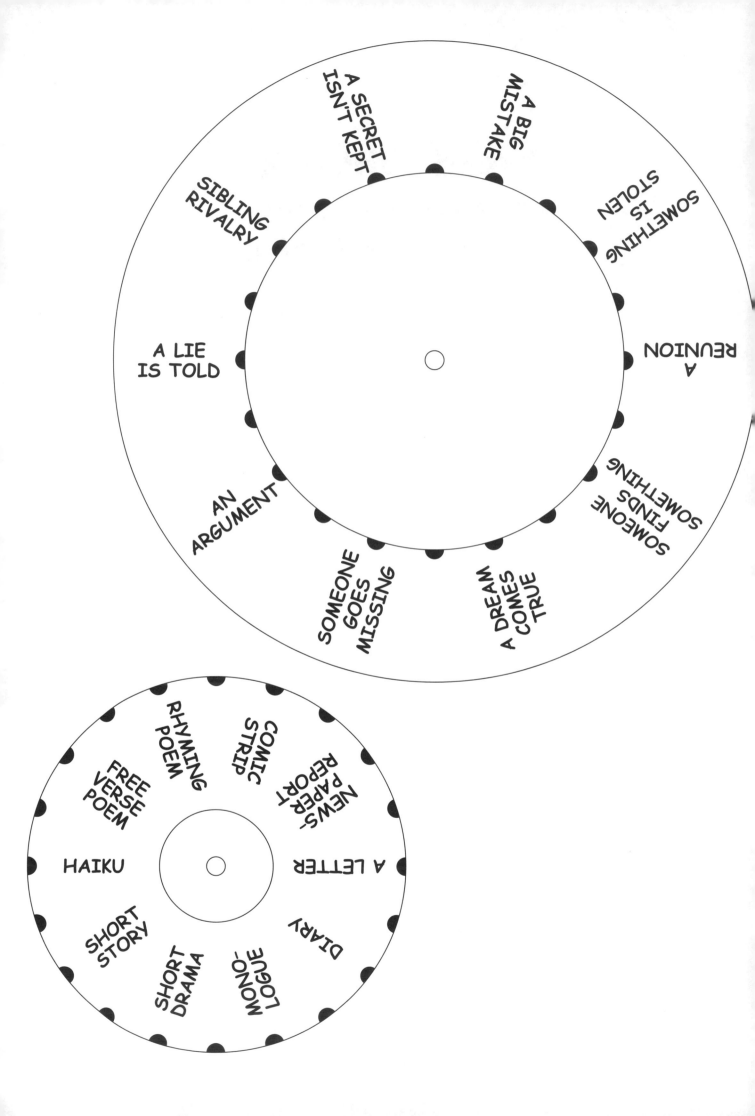

Glossary 1: Forms of Writing

This Glossary includes Fiction, Poetry and Non-fiction.

ACROSTICS – poems in which, most frequently, the letters at the start of each line spell out a word:

Shows up every Christmas without fail
Always knows what you've asked for
Never forgets where you live
Takes nothing in return:
Ace guy

AUTOBIOGRAPHICAL WRITING – a piece in which the writer tells about aspects of her/his life, memories and experiences. (See David Almond's extract from *Counting Stars* on p. 7 and Michael Rosen's poem 'Thirty-Two Lengths' on p. 9.)

BIOGRAPHICAL WRITING – a piece written by an author about another (often well known) person; such writing may well include extracts from interviews.

BOOK REVIEW – a critical report of a book, often a new one.

COMIC STRIP – a story told image by image with either dialogue and/or some accompanying prose underneath each image.

DRAMA – a piece written to be performed, usually fictional (see the extract from the stage adaptation of *Kensuke's Kingdom* on p. 26 to see how to set out dialogue and action).

FAIRY TALE – a traditional tale that was originally an oral, folk tale.

FREE VERSE – poetry that does not rhyme or follow a set rhythm. Modern free verse is often written in everyday language. (See Michael Rosen's poem 'Thirty-Two Lengths' on p. 9 and James Carter's poem 'Night Car Journey' on p. 41.)

INTERVIEW – a meeting in which one person asks another a set of prepared questions which is often recorded onto audio cassette and later written/typed out as a transcript.

KENNING – a form of list poem (usually non-rhyming) that provides a cumulative list of images and qualities of its subject. Animals are a popular theme with kennings; here is a short rhyming example of an elephant kenning:

A slow-walker
A time-taker
A deep-thinker
A big-shaker

LIST POEM – a poem that repeats a word or phrase at the beginning of each line or stanza:

There's nothing quite as
growly as a bear
There's nothing quite as
howly as a wolf
As flighty as a fish
As mighty as a bull
There's nothing quite as
growly as a bear

MINI-SAGA – a story told in exactly 50 words:

'Loss of a child'
Throughout the service she howled in lament for her daughter. Her son gripped her arm, but could offer little consolation. The mother said that to lose a child so young – one that had so much going for her – was a tragedy. So why was the girl marrying the farmer's son?

MONOLOGUE – a piece of writing or performance in which a character talks about aspects of her/his life or makes observations about the world around her/him.

NEWSPAPER ARTICLE – an article that appears in a newspaper, reporting on a recent event or situation.

NOVEL – an extended story, told in chapters, that has a cast of characters, one main plot and a number of sub-plots.

RADIO PLAY – a play written for the radio; in addition to dialogue, the play may contain linking music as well as sound effects (see the extract from the stage adaptation of *Kensuke's Kingdom* on p. 26 to see how to set out dialogue and action).

SCREENPLAY – the text for a film or television drama (see the extract from the stage adaptation of *Kensuke's Kingdom* on p. 26 to see how to set out dialogue and action).

SHAPE POETRY – poetry that plays with shapes, and often takes on the shape of the subject the poem is about, such as with this poem:

YOU DON'T GET GRIEF IF YOU BRUSH

YOUR TEETH !!!!!!!!!!!!

SHORT STORY – a fictional story that usually has one main plot and a few characters.

STORYBOARD – the scenes and images for a film or television drama represented as a comic strip, image by image. The dialogue for the image can be written below each image.

SYLLABIC POETRY:
HAIKU/TANKA/CINQUAINS – haiku is a form of poetry that originated in Japan and has 17

syllables in total. These syllables are divided into three lines as follows:
1st line: five syllables
2nd line: seven syllables
3rd line: five syllables

A tiny green frog
Sits upon a lily pad
Idly moongazing

Tanka, another form of Japanese poetry has five lines of 31 syllables:

1st line: five syllables
2nd line: seven syllables
3rd line: five syllables
4th line: seven syllables
5th line: seven syllables

A further syllabic form is the clerihew, devised by an American poet, and has five lines of 22 syllables:

1st line: two syllables
2nd line: four syllables
3rd line: six syllables
4th line: eight syllables
5th line: two syllables

RAP – a rhyming poem with a strong beat, written in rhyming couplets:

I've been over the seas, now I'm back to stay
To tell you some stuff that'll blow you away
It's a whole new thing I've been thinking about
Gonna rattle your cage before I'm out

RESEARCH – finding out information on a subject – for example, from books, CD-ROMs, libraries, the Internet or by interviewing people.

TRAVEL WRITING – a form of autobiographical writing in which the author will tell of her/his experiences either on a journey or in a place or variety of places.

Glossary 2: Useful Terms for Writing

This Glossary includes Fiction, Poetry and Non-fiction.

ALLITERATION – words close together in a line of poetry or a sentence of prose that begin with the same letters or sounds: 'We were wishing', 'Talk to Thomas'.

ASSONANCE – words close together that have similar sounds: 'Where did *Joe go*?', 'I need *four more*'.

ATMOSPHERE – how it feels to be in a certain place at a certain time in a story, poem or other form of writing.

CHARACTERS – the people in a fictional story, drama, poem or film.

CLICHÉ – an overused and unoriginal phrase or description: 'as black as night', 'as cold as ice'.

COLLOQUIAL LANGUAGE – everyday speech/language.

DIALOGUE – the speech in stories and other forms of writing as spoken by the characters – see extract from *The Nightwatchmen* on p. 33 by Helen Cresswell and the extract from the stage adaptation of *Kensuke's Kingdom* on p. 26.

DRAFTING and **EDITING** – DRAFTING = doing different versions to improve and develop a piece of writing. EDITING = checking a piece of writing for spelling, grammar, punctuation and any errors in the text.

FICTION – an invented story.

FORM – the type of fiction. For example, novel, short story, play, monologue or mini-saga – or the type of poem, such as free verse, rap or kenning, or the type of non-fiction: newspaper report, book review or interview.

GENRE – the type of fictional story. For example, fantasy, horror, science fiction or fairy tale or non-fiction – letter writing, journalism and travel writing.

IMAGERY – Tony Mitton: 'The imagery is the kind of pictures in the head the poem makes.'

'IN MEDIA RES' – when a story begins in the middle of an event or action or with a piece of dialogue.

NARRATION – FIRST PERSON: when one person, a narrator, tells the story from their point of view – that person will be the 'I . . .' in the story.

NARRATION – THIRD PERSON: when an unknown person, someone outside of the fictional world, tells a story – such as in fairy tales, 'Once upon a time in a faraway land . . .'.

NARRATIVE – the story that a book or poem tells.

NARRATOR – a person that tells a story.

PERSONIFICATION – when a metaphor compares something to a human being – 'The wind laughed', 'The sea is angry.'

PLOT – the sequence of the most important events that take place in a story; sub-plots (such as in films, dramas and novels) are the smaller events that take place.

POINT OF VIEW – some stories/poems are either narrated by one person or show the world as it is seen through one person's eyes; this is the 'point of view' of the story/poem.

PROSE – written language that is not poetry. For example, the text (including dialogue) in a short story or novel.

RHYME – when words at the end of a line have the same sounds:

> Off to the city and off to the *sea*.
> Off to the valley and back for *tea*.

A half-rhyme is when the words at the end of a line have similar sounds:

> Good for souls and hearts and *minds*.
> one book changes many *lives*.

RHYTHM – the beat and the feel of a poem, song or piece of music – which will depend upon the words used, the combination of words and the number of words in each line.

SETTING – the place(s) in which a story/poem is set.

SIMILE and **METAPHOR** – SIMILE = when you say one thing is *like* something else – 'As cunning as a fox', 'She felt trapped like a bird in a cage'; METAPHOR= when you say one thing actually <u>is</u> something else – 'It's raining nails', 'The city is a jungle tonight.'

SYNOPSIS – a short piece of writing that summarises something, such as the plot of a novel written on the back cover of a book.

THEME – the subject of a story/poem/non-fiction piece.

STRUCTURE – how a piece of writing is shaped and set out, with a beginning, middle and end.

SUSPENSE – the feeling that something is about to happen in a poem/story/film/play.

STANZA – (also known as a VERSE) a group of lines in a poem.

SYLLABLES – the individual beats in a word. Po / em has two beats. Po / et / ry has three beats. How many beats are there in your name?

VERSE – (also known as a STANZA) – a group of lines in a poem.

Recommended Books and Useful Websites

Recommended books

To Rhyme or Not to Rhyme? – Teaching children to write poetry – Sandy Brownjohn (Hodder & Stoughton)

Creating Writers – A creative writing manual for schools – James Carter (RoutledgeFalmer)

Talking Books – Children's authors talk about the craft, creativity and process of writing (including Jacqueline Wilson, Berlie Doherty, Philip Pullman, Ian Beck, Terry Deaty, Benjamin Zephaniah and Helen Cresswell) – James Carter

Rap It Up – Reading, writing and performing rap poems in the classroom – James Carter – a rap poem anthology, teacher's book and poetry/music CD (Questions Publishing)

How to Teach Fiction Writing at Key Stage 2 – Pie Corbett (David Fulton)

Catapults and Kingfishers – Teaching poetry in primary schools – Pie Corbett and Brian Moses (Oxford University Press)

My Grandmother's Motorbike – Story writing in the primary school – Pie Corbett and Brian Moses (Oxford University Press)

Writing – Kate Jones (Hodder – super.activ series)

Did I Hear You Write? – Michael Rosen (Five Leaves)

Jumpstart – Poetry in the secondary school – Cliff Yates (The Poetry Society)

The Poetry Book for Primary Schools – edited by Anthony Wilson with Sian Hughes (The Poetry Society)

Useful websites

Achuka: www.achuka.com

Poetryzone: www.poetryzone.ndirect.co.uk

The Poetry Society, London: www.poetrysoc.com

The Poetry Library, London: www.poetrylibrary.org.uk

Young ABC Tales: www.youngABCtales.com

Young Writer magazine: www.mystworld.com/youngwriter

Bibliography

All are books unless otherwise stated.

'TEXT AND THEMES' CHAPTER

Memories

Counting Stars by David Almond (Hodder Headline)
'Thirty-Two Lengths'– poem by Michael Rosen from *Quick, Let's Get Out of Here* (Scholastic)
Boy by Roald Dahl (Puffin)
Cider With Rosie by Laurie Lee (Penguin)
Zlata's Diary by Zlata Filipovic (Puffin)
The Diary of Anne Frank – Anne Frank (Puffin)

Dreams

'Elephant Dreams' – poem by Ian Mcmillan from *The Best of Ian Mcmillan* (Pan Macmillan)
'Jakey' – short story from *Badger on the Barge* by Janni Howker (Walker Books)
Bulging Brains by Nick Arnold (Scholastic)
Wolf by Gillian Cross (Puffin and Oxford University Press)
Bill's New Frock by Anne Fine (Puffin)
'Metamorphosis' – short story by Franz Kafka (Penguin)

School

Tough Luck by Berlie Doherty (Collins)
The Twins at St Clare's/Mallory Towers by Enid Blyton (Egmont)
Harry Potter series by J. K. Rowling (Bloomsbury)
Hard Times by Charles Dickens (Penguin)
The Demon Headmaster by Gillian Cross (Puffin and Oxford University Press)
Please Mrs Butler and *I Heard It In the Playground* by Allan Ahlberg (Puffin)

Friendships

A Monkey's Wedding by Norman Silver (Faber & Faber)

The Blue Horse by Norman Silver (Faber & Faber)

Kensuke's Kingdom – Vicky Ireland's stage adaptation of Michael Morpurgo's original novel (Mammoth)

Farm Boy by Michael Morpurgo (Collins)

His Dark Materials by Philip Pullman (Scholastic/David Fickling Books)

Toy Story / Toy Story 2 – films, directed by John Lassetter – theme song 'You've Got a Friend in Me' by Randy Newman

TV series – *Neighbours* and *Byker Grove* (both BBC) *Hollyoaks* (C4)

Skellig by David Almond (Hodder Headline)

Kit's Wilderness by David Almond (Hodder)

Cagney and Lacey – American TV series

Starsky and Hutch – American TV series

Inspector Morse – Carlton TV series

Sherlock Holmes stories by Arthur Conan Doyle (Penguin)

Tintin series by Hergé (Methuen)

Noughts & Crosses by Malorie Blackman (Transworld)

Romeo and Juliet by William Shakespeare

Outsiders

The Adventures of Tom Sawyer by Mark Twain (Penguin)

The Nightwatchmen by Helen Cresswell (Hodder)

The Story of Tracy Beaker, The Suitcase Kid, The Dare Game by Jacqueline Wilson (Transworld)

Toy Story – film, directed by John Lassetter

The Jungle Book – film, Disney

Skellig by David Almond (Hodder Headline)

Harry Potter series by J. K. Rowling (Bloomsbury)

A Midsummer's Nights Dream by William Shakespeare

Journeys

'Night Car Journey' – poem by James Carter from *Cars Stars Electric Guitars* (Walker Books)

Witch Child by Celia Rees (Bloomsbury)

The Canterbury Tales by Geoffrey Chaucer

Gulliver's Travels by Jonathan Swift (Penguin)

Treasure Island by Robert Louis Stevenson (Penguin)

The Hobbit by J. R. R. Tolkein

His Dark Materials by Philip Pullman (Scholastic/David Fickling Books)

Where the Wild Things Are by Maurice Sendak (Puffin)

Dear Olly by Michael Morpurgo (Collins)

Waiting for Anya by Michael Morpurgo (Egmont)

Kensuke's Kingdom by Michael Morpurgo (Collins)
Billy the Kid by Michael Morpurgo (Pavilion)
The Straight Story – film, directed by David Lynch
Around Ireland with a Fridge by Tony Hawks (Ebury Press)
'The Swimmer' – short story by John Cleever (Vintage)

Time

The Time Traveller by Alison Uttley (Puffin)
'Four o' clock Friday' – poem by John Foster from *Four o'clock Friday* (Oxford University Press)
The Time Machine by H. G. Wells (Penguin)
Tom's Midnight Garden by Philippa Pearce (Puffin)
Thief! by Malorie Blackman (Transworld)
'Child From the Future' – poem by Tony Mitton from *Plum* (Scholastic)
'Time' – song by Pink Floyd from CD *The Dark Side of the Moon* (EMI)
Horrible Histories series (Scholastic) by Terry Deary (including *The Rotten Romans, The Vile Victorians, Wicked Words* and *The Savage Stone Age*)

IN 'IMAGES' CHAPTER

The Trokeville Way by Russell Hoban (Jonathon Cape)
Ian Beck's picture books are published by Scholastic, David Fickling Books, Transworld and Orchard Books.
'Recycling Rap' by John Foster from *Standing on the Sidelines* (Oxford University Press)
The Last Wolf by Michael Morpurgo (Transworld)

IN 'MUSIC' CHAPTER

Midnight Man by Berlie Doherty, illustrated by Ian Andrew (Walker Books)
Blue John by Berlie Doherty, illustrated by Tim Clarey (Puffin)
Fantasia – film (Walt Disney, 1941)
Jaws – film (Stephen Spielburg, 1975)
Psycho – film (Alfred Hitchcock, 1960)